GRADES 3–5

Differentiating Instruction With Menus

Social Studies

Differentiating Instruction With Menus

Social Studies

Laurie E. Westphal

PRUFROCK PRESS INC.
WACO, TEXAS

Library of Congress Cataloging-in-Publication Data

Westphal, Laurie E., 1967–
  Differentiating instruction with menus. Social studies / Laurie E. Westphal.
     p. cm.
  Includes bibliographical references.
  ISBN-13: 978-1-59363-228-1 (pbk.)
  ISBN-10: 1-59363-228-2 (pbk.)
  1. Social sciences—Study and teaching—United States. I. Title.
  H62.5.U5W47 2007
  300.71'073—dc22
                          2007016525

Edited by Jennifer Robins
Production Design by Marjorie Parker

ISBN-13: 978-1-59363-228-1
ISBN-10: 1-59363-228-2

Prufrock Press Inc.
P.O. Box 8813
Waco, TX 76714-8813
Phone: (800) 998-2208
Fax: (800) 240-0333
http://www.prufrock.com

CONTENTS

CHAPTER 1

Choice

"**O**h my gosh! THAAAAANK YOU!" exclaimed one of my students as he fell to his knees dramatically in the middle of my classroom. I had just handed out a List Menu on the periodic table and told my students they would be able to choose how they wanted to learn the material.

Why Is Choice Important?

Ask adults whether they would prefer to choose what to do or be told what to do, and of course, they are going to say they would prefer to have a choice. Students have the same feelings. Although they may not stand up and demand a choice if none is present, they benefit in many ways from having them.

One benefit of choice is its ability to meet the needs of so many different students and their learning styles. The Dunedin College of Education (Keen, 2001) conducted a research study on the preferred learning styles of 250 gifted students. Students were asked to rank different learning options. Of the 13 different options described to the students, only one option did not receive at least one negative response, and that was the option of having choice. Although all students have different learning styles and preferences, choice is the one option that meets all students' needs. Students are going to choose what best fits their learning styles and educational needs.

> **" . . . I am different in the way I do stuff. I like to build stuff with my hands. . . ."**
>
> *—Sixth-grade student, when asked why he enjoyed activities that allow choice.*

Another benefit of choice is a greater sense of independence for the students. What a powerful feeling! Students will be designing and creating a product based on what they envision, rather than what their teacher envisions. When students would enter my middle-school classroom, they often had been trained by previous teachers to produce exactly what the teacher wanted, not what the students thought would be best. Teaching my students that what they envision could be correct (and wonderful) was often a struggle. "Is this what you want?" or "Is this right?" were popular questions as we started the school year. Allowing students to have choices in the products they create to show their learning helps create independence at an early age.

Strengthened student focus on the required content is a third benefit. When students have choices in the activities they wish to complete, they are more focused on the learning that leads to their choice product. Students become excited when they learn information that can help them develop a product they would like to create. Students pay close attention to instruction and have an immediate application for the knowledge being presented in class. Also, if students are focused, they are less likely to be off task during instruction.

Many a great educator has referred to the idea that the best learning takes place when the students have a desire to learn. Some students have a desire to learn anything that is new to them; others do not want to learn anything unless it is of interest to them. By incorporating different activities from which to choose, students stretch beyond what they already know, and teachers create a void that needs to be filled. This void leads to a desire to learn.

How Can Teachers Provide Choices?

When people go to a restaurant, the common goal is to find something on the menu to satisfy their hunger. Students come into our classrooms having a hunger, as well—a hunger for learning. Choice menus are a way of allowing our students to choose how they would like to satisfy that hunger. At the very least, a menu is a list of choices that students use to choose an activity (or activities) they would like to complete to show what they have learned. At best, it is a complex system in which students earn points by making choices from different areas of study. All menus should also incorporate a free-choice option for those "picky eaters" who would like to make a special order to satisfy their learning hunger.

The next few sections provide examples of the main types of menus that will be used in this book. Each menu has its own benefits, limitations or drawbacks, and time considerations. An explanation of the free-choice option and its management will follow the information on each type of menu.

Tic-Tac-Toe Menu

Description

The Tic-Tac-Toe Menu (see Figure 1.1) is a basic menu that contains a total of eight predetermined choices and one free choice for students.

All choices are created at the same level of Bloom's Revised taxonomy (Anderson et al., 2001). Each choice carries the same weight for grading and has similar expectations for completion time and effort.

Benefits

Flexibility. This menu can cover one topic in depth or three different objectives. When this menu covers just one objective, students have the option of completing three projects in a tic-tac-toe pattern, or simply picking three from the menu. When it covers three objectives, students will need to complete a tic-tac-toe pattern (one in each column or row) to be sure they have completed one activity from each objective.

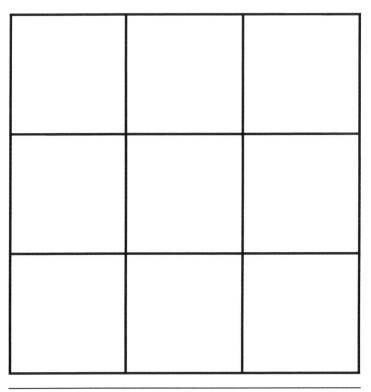

Figure 1.1. Tic-tac-toe menu

Friendly Design. Students quickly understand how to use this menu.

Weighting. All projects are equally weighted, so recording grades and maintaining paperwork is easily accomplished with this menu.

Limitations

Few Topics. These menus only cover one or three topics.

Short Time Period. They are intended for shorter periods of time, between 1–3 weeks.

Student Compromise. Although this menu does allow choice, a student will sometimes have to compromise and complete an activity he or she would not have chosen because it completes the required tic-tac-toe. (This is not always bad, though!)

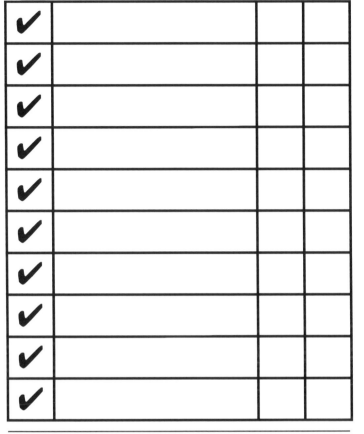

Figure 1.2. List menu

Time Considerations

These menus are usually intended for shorter amounts of completion time—at the most, they should take 3 weeks. If it focuses on one topic in depth, the menu can be completed in one week.

List Menu

Description

The List Menu (see Figure 1.2), or Challenge List, is a more complex menu than the Tic-Tac-Toe Menu, with a total of at least 10 predetermined choices, each with its own point value, and at least one free choice for students. Choices are simply listed with assigned points based on the levels of Bloom's Revised taxonomy. The choices carry different weights and have different expectations for completion time and effort. A point criterion is set forth that equals 100%, and students choose how they wish to attain that point goal.

Benefits

Responsibility. Students have complete control over their grades. They really like the idea that they can guarantee their grade if they complete the required work. If they lose points on one of the chosen assignments, they can complete another to be sure they have met their goal points.

Concept Reinforcement. This menu also allows for an in-depth study of material; however, with the different levels of Bloom's Revised taxonomy being represented, students who are still learning the concepts can choose some of the lower level point value projects to reinforce the basics before jumping into the higher level activities.

Limitations

Few Topics. This menu is best used for one topic in depth, although it can be used for up to three different topics, as well.

Cannot Guarantee Objectives. If it is used for three topics, it is possible for a student to not have to complete an activity for each objective, depending on the choices he or she makes.

Preparation. Teachers need to have all materials ready at the beginning of the unit for students to be able to choose any of the activities on the list, which requires advance planning.

Time Considerations

The List Menus are usually intended for shorter amounts of completion time—at the most, 2 weeks.

2-5-8 Menu

> ## "My favorite menu is the 2-5-8 kind. It's easy to understand and I can pick just what I want to do."
>
> *—Fourth-grade student, when asked about his favorite type of menu.*

Description

A 2-5-8 Menu (see Figure 1.3) is a variation of the List Menu, with a total of at least eight predetermined choices: at least two choices with a point value of two, at least four choices with a point value of five, and at least two choices with a point value of eight. Choices are assigned points based on the levels of Bloom's Revised taxonomy (Anderson et al., 2001). Choices with a point value of two represent the *remember* and *understand* levels, choices with a point value of five represent the *apply* and *analyze* levels, and choices with a point value of eight represent the *evaluate* and *create* levels. All levels of choices carry different weights and have different expectations for completion time and effort. Students are expected to earn 10 points for a 100%.

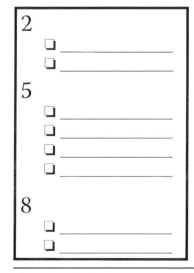

Figure 1.3. 2-5-8 menu

Students choose what combination they would like to use to attain that point goal.

Benefits

Responsibility. With this menu, students still have complete control over their grades.

Guaranteed Activity. This menu's design is also set up in such a way that students must complete at least one activity at a higher level of Bloom's Revised taxonomy in order to reach their point goal.

Limitations

One Topic. Although it can be used for more than one topic, this menu works best with in-depth study of one topic.

No Free Choice. By nature, it does not allow students to propose their own free choice, because point values need to be assigned based on Bloom's Revised taxonomy.

Higher Level Thinking. Students will complete only one activity at a higher level of thinking.

Time Considerations

The 2-5-8 Menus are usually intended for a shorter amount of completion time—at the most, one week.

Game Show Menu

"This menu really challenged my students. If one of my students saw another student choosing a more difficult option, they wanted to choose one, too. I had very few students choose the basic options on this menu. It was wonderful!"

—Sixth-grade science teacher

Description

The Game Show Menu (see Figure 1.4) is the most complex menu. It covers multiple topics or objectives with at least three predetermined choices and a free student choice for each objective. Choices are assigned points based on the levels of Bloom's taxonomy. All choices carry different weights and have different expectations for completion time and effort. A point criterion is set forth that equals 100%. Students must complete at least one activity from each objective in order to reach their goal.

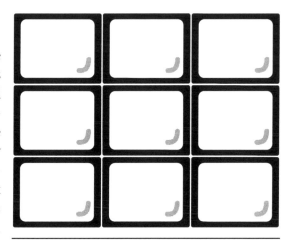

Figure 1.4. Game show menu

Benefits

Free Choice. This menu allows many choices for students, but if they do not want to complete the offered activities, they can propose their own activity for each objective.

Responsibility. This menu also allows students to guarantee their own grades.

Different Learning Levels. It also has the flexibility to allow for individualized contracts for different learning levels within the classroom. Each student can contract for a certain number of points for his or her grade.

Objectives Guaranteed. The teacher is also guaranteed that the students complete an activity from each objective covered, even if it is at a lower level.

Limitations

Confirm Expectations. The only real limitation here is that students (and parents) must understand the guidelines for completing the menu.

Time Considerations

These menus are usually intended for a longer amount of completion time. Although they can be used as a yearlong menu (each column could be a grading period), they are usually intended for 4–6 weeks.

Free Choice

> " . . . the free choice. I love it, love it!!! I got to do what I really wanted to! [The teacher] let me reserch [sic] my own book."
>
> —*Second-grade student, when asked what she liked most about the menu students had just completed.*

With most of the menus, the students are allowed to submit a free choice for their teacher's consideration. Figure 1.5 shows two sample proposal forms that have been used many times successfully in my classroom. The form used is based on the type of menu being presented. If students are using the Tic-Tac-Toe Menu, there is no need to submit a point proposal. A copy of these forms should be given to each student when each menu is first introduced. A discussion should be held with the students so they understand the expectations of a free choice. If students do not want to make a proposal using the proposal form after the teacher has discussed the entire menu and its activities, they can place the unused form in a designated place in the classroom. Others may want to use their form, and it is often surprising who wants to submit a proposal form after hearing about the opportunity!

Proposal forms must be submitted before students begin working on their free-choice products. The teacher then knows what the students are working on and the student knows the expectations the teacher has for that product. Once approved, the forms can easily be stapled to the student's menu sheet. The students can refer to it as they develop their free-choice product, and when the grading takes place, the teacher can refer to the agreement for the "graded" features of the product.

Each part of the proposal form is important and needs to be discussed with students:

- *Name/Teacher's Approval.* The student must submit this form to the teacher for approval. The teacher will carefully review all of the information, send it back to the student for correction, if needed, and then sign the top.
- *Points Requested.* Found only on the point-based menu proposal form, this is usually where negotiation needs to take place. Students usually will submit their first request for a very high number (even the 100% goal.) They really do equate the amount of time something

Name _____ Teacher's Approval: _____

Free-Choice Proposal Form for Point-Based Menu

Points Requested: _____ Points Approved: _____

<u>Proposal Outline</u>

1. What specific topic or idea will you learn about?

2. What criteria should be used to grade it? (Neatness, content, creativity, artistic value, etc.)

3. What will your product look like?

4. What materials will you need from the teacher to create this product?

Name _____ Teacher's Approval: _____

Free-Choice Proposal Form

<u>Proposal Outline</u>

1. What specific topic or idea will you learn about?

2. What criteria should be used to grade it? (Neatness, content, creativity, artistic value, etc.)

3. What will your product look like?

4. What materials will you need from the teacher to create this product?

Figure 1.5. Sample proposal forms

will take with the amount of points it should earn. But, please note, the points are *always* based on the levels of Bloom's Revised taxonomy. For example, a PowerPoint presentation with a vocabulary word quiz would get minimal points, although it may have taken a long time to create. If the students have not been exposed to the levels of Bloom's Revised taxonomy, this can be difficult to explain. You can always refer to the popular "Bloom's Verbs" to help explain the difference between time requirements and higher level activities.

- *Points Approved.* Found only on the point-based menu proposal form, this is the final decision recorded by the teacher once the point haggling is finished.

- *Proposal Outline.* This is where the student will tell you everything about the product he or she intends to complete. These questions should be completed in such a way that you can really picture what the student is planning on completing. This also shows you that the student knows what he or she is planning on completing.

  - *What specific topic or idea will you learn about?* Students need to be specific here. It is not acceptable to write *science* or *reading*. This is where they look at the objectives of the project and choose which objective their project demonstrates.

  - *What criteria should be used to grade it?* Although there are rubrics for all of the projects that the students might create, it is important for the students to explain what criteria are most important to evaluate the product. The student may indicate that the rubric being used for all the predetermined projects is fine; however, he or she may also want to add other criteria here.

  - *What will your product look like?* It is important that this be as detailed as possible. If a student cannot express what it will "look like," he or she has probably not given the free-choice plan enough thought.

  - *What materials will you need from the teacher to create this product?* This is an important consideration. Sometimes students do not have the means to purchase items for their project. This can be negotiated, as well, but if you ask what students may need, they often will develop even grander ideas for their free choice.

CHAPTER 2

How to Use Menus in the Classroom

There are different ways to use instructional menus in the classroom. In order to decide how to implement each menu, the following questions should be considered: How much prior knowledge of the topic being taught do the students have before the unit or lesson begins and how much information is readily available for students to obtain on their own?

There are three customary ways to use menus in the classroom. Using them for enrichment and supplementary activities is the most common. In this case, the students usually do not have a lot of background knowledge and the information about the topic may not be readily available to all students. The teacher will introduce the menu and the activities at the beginning of a unit. The teacher will then progress through the content at the normal rate, using his or her own curricular materials and periodically allowing class time and homework time throughout the unit for students to work on their menu choices to supplement a deeper understanding of the lessons being taught. This method is very effective, as it builds in an immediate use for the content the teacher is covering. For example, at the beginning of a unit on the Civil War, the teacher many introduce the menu with the explanation that students may not have all of the knowledge to complete all of their choices yet. During the unit, however, more content will be provided and they will be prepared to work on new choices. If students want to work ahead, they certainly can find the information on their own, but that is not required. Gifted students often see this as a challenge and will begin to investigate concepts mentioned in the menu before the teacher discusses them. This helps build an immense pool of background knowledge before the topic is even discussed in the classroom. As teachers, we fight the battle of having students read ahead or "come to class prepared to discuss." By introducing a menu at the beginning of a unit and allowing students to complete products as instruction progresses, the students naturally investigate the information and come to class prepared without it being a completely separate requirement.

Another option for using menus in the classroom is to replace certain curricular activities the teacher uses to teach the specified content. In this case, the students may have some limited background knowledge about the content and information is readily available for them in their classroom resources. The teacher would pick and choose which aspects of the content must be directly taught to the students, and which could be appropriately learned and reinforced through product menus. The unit is then designed using both formal instructional lessons and specific menu days where the students will use the menu to reinforce the prior knowledge they already have learned. In order for this option to be effective, the teacher must feel very comfortable with the students' prior knowledge level. Another variation on this method is using the menus to drive center or station activities. Centers have many different functions in the classroom—most importantly reinforcing the instruction that has taken place. Rather than having a set rotation for centers, the teacher could use the menu activities as enrichment or supplementary activities during center time for those students who need more than just reinforcement; centers could be set up with the materials students would need to complete various products.

The third option for menu use is the use of mini-lessons, with the menus driving the accompanying classroom activities. This method is best used when the majority of the students have a lot of prior knowledge about the topic. The teacher can design 10–15 minute mini-lessons, where students quickly review basic concepts that are already familiar to them. The students are then turned loose to choose an activity on the menu to show they understand the concept. The game show menu usually works very well with this method of instruction, as the topics across the top usually lend themselves to the mini-lessons. It is important that the students have prior knowledge on the content because the lesson cycle is cut very short in this use of menus. Using menus in this way does not allow teachers to use the guided practice step of the lesson, as it is assumed the students already understand the information. The teacher is simply reviewing the information and then moving right to the higher levels of Bloom's Revised taxonomy by asking students to create a product. By using the menus in this way, the teacher avoids the "I already know this" glossy looks from his or her students. Another important consideration is the independence level of the students. In order for this use of menus to be effective, students will need to be able to work independently for up to 30 minutes after the mini-lesson. Because students are often interested in the product they have chosen, this is not a critical issue, but still one worth mentioning as teachers consider how they would like to use various menus in their classroom.

CHAPTER 3

Guidelines for Products

> ## "... each project is unique."
>
> *—Fifth-grade student, when asked why he enjoys choice menus.*

This chapter outlines the different types of products included in the featured menus, as well as the guidelines and expectations for each. It is very important that students know exactly what the expectations of a completed product are when they choose to work on it. By discussing these expectations *before* students begin and having the information readily available ahead of time, you will limit the frustration on everyone's part.

$1 Contract

Consideration should be given to the cost of creating the products featured on any menu. The resources available to students vary within a classroom, and students should not be graded on the amount of materials they can purchase to make a product look better. These menus are designed to equalize the resources students have available. The materi-

---

$1 Contract

I did not spend more than $1.00 on my _____.

_____   _____
Student Signature   Date

My child, _____, did not spend more than $1.00 on the product he or she created.

_____   _____
Parent Signature   Date

Figure 3.1. $1 contract

als for most products are available for less than a dollar and can often be found in a teacher's classroom as part of the classroom supplies. If a product requires materials from the student, there is a $1 contract as part of the product criteria. This is a very important piece in the explanation of the product. First of all, by limiting the amount of money a child can spend, it creates an equal amount of resources for all students. Second, it actually encourages a more creative product. When students are limited by the amount of materials they can readily purchase, they often have to use materials from home in new and unique ways. Figure 3.1 is a sample of the contract that has been used many times in my classroom with various products.

The Products

Table 3.1 contains a list of the products used in this book. These products were chosen for their flexibility in meeting learning styles, as well as for being products many teachers are already using in their classroom. They have been arranged by learning style—visual, kinesthetic, or auditory—and each menu has been designed to include products from all of the learning styles. Of course, some of the products may be listed in more than one area depending on how they are presented or implemented. The specific expectations for all of the products are presented in an easy-to-

Table 3.1
Products

Visual	Kinesthetic	Auditory
Acrostic	Commercial	Commercial
Advertisement	Concentration Cards	Interview
Book Cover	Diorama	News Report
Brochure/Pamphlet	Flipbook	Play
Cartoon/Comic Strip	Game	PowerPoint— Presentation
Collage	Mobile	
Crossword Puzzle	Model	Puppet
Greeting Card	Play	Song/Rap
Letter	Product Cube	Speech
Map	Puppet	Student-Taught Lesson
Mind Map	Student-Taught Lesson	Video
Newspaper Article	Three-Dimensional Timeline	You Be the Person Presentation
Poster	Video	
PowerPoint— Stand Alone		
Questionnaire		
Recipe/Recipe Card		
Scrapbook		
Story		
Trading Cards		
Venn Diagram		
Video		
Window Pane		
Worksheet		

read card format that can be reproduced for students (see Figure 3.2). This format is convenient for students to have in front of them when they work on their projects. These cards also can be laminated and posted on a bulletin board for easy access during classroom work.

Acrostic	Advertisement	Book Cover
• At least 8.5" x 11" • Neatly written or typed • Target word will be written down the left side of the paper • Each descriptive word chosen must begin with one of the letters from the target word • Each descriptive word chosen must be related to the target word	• At least 8.5" x 11" • A slogan should be included • Color picture of item or service • Include price, if appropriate • Can be developed on the computer	• Front Cover—title, author, and image • Cover Inside Flap—summary of the book • Back Inside Flap—brief biography of the author • Back Cover—editorial comments about the book • Spine—title and author
Brochure/Pamphlet	**Cartoon/Comic Strip**	**Collage**
• At least 8.5" x 11" • Must be in three-fold format; front fold has the title and picture • Must have both pictures and written text • Information should be in paragraph form with at least five facts included	• At least 8.5" x 11" • Should have at least six cells • Must have meaningful dialogue • Must include color	• At least 8.5" x 11" • Pictures must be neatly cut from magazines or newspapers (no clip art) • Label items as required in task
Commercial	**Concentration Cards**	**Crossword Puzzle**
• Must be 5–10 minutes in length • Script must be turned in before commercial is presented • Can be presented live to an audience or recorded • Props or some form of costume must be used • Can include more than one person	• At least 20 index cards (10 matching sets) must be made • Both pictures and words can be used • Information should be placed on just one side of each card • Include an answer key that shows the matches • All cards must be submitted in a carrying bag	• At least 20 significant words or phrases should be included • Develop appropriate clues • Include puzzle and answer key
Diorama	**Flipbook**	**Game**
• At least 4" x 5" x 8" • Must be self-standing • All interior space must be covered with relevant pictures and information • Name written on the back in permanent ink • Informational/title card attached to diorama	• At least 8.5" x 11" folded in half • All information or opinions are supported by facts • Created with the correct number of flaps cut into the top • Color is optional • Name must be written on the back	• At least four thematic game pieces • At least 25 colored/thematic squares • At least 20 question/activity cards • Include a thematic title on the board • Include a complete set of rules for playing the game • At least the size of an open file folder (11" x 17")

Figure 3.2. Product guidelines

Greeting Card	Interview	Letter
• Front—colored pictures, words optional • Front Inside—personal note related to topic • Back Inside—greeting or saying; must meet product criteria • Back Outside—logo, publisher, and price for card	• Must have at least five questions relevant to the topic being studied • Questions and answers must be neatly written or typed	• Neatly written or typed • Uses proper letter format • At least three paragraphs in length • Must follow type of letter stated in the menu (e.g., friendly, persuasive, informational)
Map	**Mind Map**	**Mobile**
• At least 8.5" x 11" • Accurate information is included • Includes at least 10 relevant locations • Includes compass rose, legend, scale, and key	• At least 8.5" x 11" • Must have one central idea • Follow the "no more than four" rule—no more than four words coming from any one word	• At least 10 pieces of related information • Includes color and pictures • Has at least three layers of hanging information • Hangs in a balanced way
Model	**News Report**	**Newspaper Article**
• At least 8" x 8" x 12" • Parts of model must be labeled, and should be in scale when appropriate • Must include a title card • Name written on model in ink	• Must address the who, what, where, when, why, and how of the topic • Script of report turned in with project, or before if performance will be "live" • Must be either performed live or recorded	• Must be informational in nature • Must follow standard newspaper format • Must include picture with caption that supports article • At least three paragraphs in length • Neatly written or typed
Play	**Poster**	**PowerPoint—Stand Alone**
• Must be between 5–10 minutes long • Script must be turned in before play is presented • Must be presented to an audience • Should have props or some form of costume • Can include more than one person	• Should be the size of a standard poster board • Includes at least five pieces of important information • Must have title • Must contain both words and pictures • Name must be written on the back	• At least 10 informational slides and one title slide with student's name • No more than 15 words per page • Slides must have color and at least one graphic per page • Animation is optional, and should not distract from information being presented

Figure 3.2. Product guidelines

PowerPoint—Presentation	Product Cube	Puppet
• At least 10 informational slides and one title slide with student's name • No more than 15 words per page • Slides must have color and at least one graphic per page • Animation is optional, and should not distract from information being presented • Presentation should be timed and flow with the oral presentation	• All six sides of the cube must be filled with information • Name must be printed neatly at the bottom of one of the sides of the cube	• Puppet should be handmade and must have a moveable mouth • A list of supplies used to make the puppet must be turned in with the puppet • If used in a play, all play criteria must be met, as well.
Questionnaire	**Recipe/Recipe Card**	**Scrapbook**
• Neatly written or typed • Includes at least 10 questions with possible answers, and at least one question that requires a written response • Questions must be helpful to gathering information on the topic being studied	• Must be written neatly or typed on a piece of paper or an index card • Must have a list of ingredients with measurements for each • Must have numbered steps that explain how to make the recipe	• Cover of scrapbook must have a meaningful title and the student's name • Must have at least five themed pages • Each page will have at least one picture • All photos will have captions
Song/Rap	**Speech**	**Story**
• Words must make sense • Can be presented to an audience or taped • Written words will be turned in before performance or with taped song • Should be at least 2 minutes in length	• Must be at least 2 minutes in length • Should not be read from written paper • Note cards can be used • Written speech must be turned in before speech is presented • Voice must be clear, loud, and easy to understand	• Must be neatly written or typed • Must have all of the elements of a well-written story (setting, characters, problem, events, and solution) • Must be appropriate length to allow for story elements
Three-Dimensional Timeline	**Trading Cards**	**Venn Diagram**
• Must be no bigger than a standard-size poster board • Should be divided into equal time units • Must contain at least 10 important dates and have at least two sentences explaining why each date is important • Must have an meaningful, creative object securely attached beside each date to represent that date • Must be able to explain how each object represents each date	• Includes at least 10 cards • Each card should be at least 3" x 5" • Each should have a colored picture • Includes at least three facts on the subject of the card • Cards must have information on both sides • All cards must be submitted in a carrying bag	• At least 8.5" x 11" • Shapes should be thematic and neatly drawn • Must have a title for the entire diagram and a title for each section • Must have at least six items in each section of the diagram • Name must be written on the back of the paper

Figure 3.2. Product guidelines

Video	Window Pane	Worksheet
• Use VHS or DVD format • Turn in a written plan or storyboard with project • Students will need to arrange their own video recorder or allow teacher at least 3 days notice for use of video recorder • Covers important information about the project • Name must be written on video label	• At least 8.5" x 11" • At least six squares • Each square must include both a picture and words • Name should be recorded on the bottom righthand corner of the front of the window pane	• Must be 8.5" x 11" • Neatly written or typed • Must cover the specific topic or question in detail • Must be creative in design • Must have at least one graphic • An answer key will be turned in with the worksheet
You Be the Person Presentation • Take on the role of the person • Cover at least five important facts about his or her life • Presentation should be 3–5 minutes in length • Script must be turned in prior to the presentation • Should be prepared to answer questions from the audience while in character • Must have props or a costume		

Figure 3.2. Product guidelines

CHAPTER 4

Rubrics

> "All the grading of the projects kept me from using menus before. The rubric makes it easier though and they [the different projects] are fun to see."
>
> —*Fourth-grade teacher,*
> *when asked to explain reservations about using menus.*

The most common reason teachers feel uncomfortable with menus is the need for equal grading. Teachers often feel it is easier to grade the same type of product made by all of the students, rather than grading a large number of different products, none of which looks like any other. The great equalizer for hundreds of different products is a generic rubric that can cover all of the important qualities of an excellent product.

All-Purpose Rubric

Figure 4.1 is an example of a rubric that has been classroom tested with various menus. This rubric can be used with any point value activity

Name:_____

All-Purpose Product Rubric

Criteria	Excellent Full Credit	Good Half Credit	Poor No Credit	Self
Content: Is the content of the product well chosen?	Content chosen represents the best choice for the product. Graphics are well chosen and related to content.	Information or graphics are related to content, but are not the best choice for the product.	Information or graphics presented does not appear to be related to topic or task.	
Completeness: Is everything included in the product?	All information needed is included. Product meets the product criteria and the criteria of the task as stated.	Some important information is missing. Product meets the product criteria and the criteria of the task as stated.	Most important information is missing. The product does not meet the task, or does not meet the product criteria.	
Creativity: Is the product original?	Presentation of information is from a new perspective. Graphics are original. Product includes an element of fun and interest.	Presentation of information is from a new perspective. Graphics are not original. Product has elements of fun and interest.	There is no evidence of new thoughts or perspectives in the product.	
Correctness: Is all the information included correct?	All information presented in the product is correct and accurate.	N/A	Any portion of the information presented in the product is incorrect.	
Appropriate Communication: Is the information in the product well communicated?	All information is neat and easy to read. Product is in appropriate format and shows significant effort. Oral presentations are easy to understand and presented with fluency.	Most of the product is neat and easy to read. Product is in appropriate format and shows significant effort. Oral presentations are easy to understand, with some fluency.	The product is not neat and easy to read or the product is not in the appropriate format. It does not show significant effort. Oral presentation was not fluent or easy to understand.	
			Total Grade:	

Figure 4.1. All-purpose product rubric

presented in a menu. When a menu is presented to students, this rubric can be reproduced on the back of the menu with its guidelines. It can also be given to students to keep in their folder with their product cards so they always know the expectations as they complete projects throughout the school year. The first time students see this rubric, it should be explained in detail, especially the last column titled *self*. It is very important that students self-evaluate their projects. This column can provide a unique perspective of the project as it is being graded. Note: This rubric was designed to be specific enough that students will know the criteria the teacher is seeking, but general enough that they can still be as creative as they like in the creation of their product.

Student-Taught Lessons and Student Presentation Rubrics

Although the generic rubric can be used for all activities, there are two occasions that seem to warrant a special rubric: student-taught lessons and student presentations. These are unique situations, with many fine details that should be considered separately.

Teachers often would like to allow students to teach their fellow classmates, but are not comfortable with the grading aspect of the assignment. The student-taught lesson rubric helps focus the student on the important aspects of a well-designed lesson, and allows teachers to make the evaluation a little more subjective. The student-taught lesson rubric (see Figure 4.2) included for these menus is appropriate for all levels.

Another area that can be difficult to evaluate is student presentations. The first consideration is that of objectivity. The objectivity can be addressed through a very specific presentation rubric that states the expectations for the speaker. The rubric will need to be discussed before the students begin preparing presentations and various criteria needs to be demonstrated. The second consideration is that of the audience and its interest. It can be frustrating to have to grade 30 presentations when the audience is not paying attention, off task, or tuning out. This can be solved by allowing your audience to be directly involved in the presentation. All of the students have been instructed on the oral presentation rubric (see Figure 4.3), so when they receive their own rubric to give feedback to their classmates, they are quite comfortable with the criteria. Students are asked to rank their classmates on a scale of 1–10 in the areas of content, flow, and the prop they chose to enhance their

Student-Taught Lesson Grading Rubric   Name _____

Parts of Lesson	Excellent	Good	Fair	Poor	Self
Prepared and Ready: All materials and lesson ready at start of class period, from warm-up to conclusion of lesson.	10 Everything is ready to present.	6 Lesson is present, but small amount of scrambling.	3 Lesson is present, but major scrambling.	0 No lesson ready or missing major components.	
Understanding: Presenter understands the material well. Students understand information presented.	20 Presenter understands; almost all of the students understand information.	12 Presenter understands; 25% of students do not.	4 Presenter understands; 50% of students do not.	0 Presenter is confused.	
Completion: Includes all significant information from section or topic.	15 Includes all important information.	10 Includes most important information.	2 Includes less than 50% of the important information.	0 Information is not related.	
Practice: Includes some way for students to practice or access the information.	20 Practice present, well chosen.	10 Practice present, can be applied effectively.	5 Practice present, not related or best choice.	0 No practice or students are confused.	
Interest/Fun: Most of the class involved, interested, and participating.	15 Everyone interested and participating.	10 75% actively participating.	5 Less than 50% actively participating.	0 Everyone off task.	
Creativity: Information presented in imaginative way.	20 Wow, creative! I never would have thought of that!	12 Good ideas!	5 Some good pieces but general instruction.	0 No creativity; all lecture/ notes/ worksheet.	
				Total Grade:	

Your Topic/Objective:

Comments:

Don't Forget:
All copy requests and material requests must be made at least 24 hours in advance.

Figure 4.2. Student-taught lesson grading rubric

presentation (see Figure 4.4). They are also asked to state two things the presenter did well. Although most students understand this should be a positive experience for the presenter, it may want to be reinforced that some notes are not necessary on their peer rankings; for example, if the presenter dropped his or her product and had to pick it up, the presenter knows this and it probably does not need to be noted again. The feedback should be positive and specific, as well. A comment of "Great!" is not what should be recorded; instead, something specific such as "I could hear you speak loudly and clearly throughout the entire presentation," or "You had great graphics!" should be written on the form. These types of comments really make the students take note and feel great about their presentations. The teacher should not be surprised to note that the students often look through all of their classmates' feedback and comments before ever consulting the rubric the teacher completed. Once students have completed a feedback form for a presenter, the forms can then be gathered at the end of each presentation, stapled together, and given to the presenter at the end of the class.

Name:_____

Oral Presentation Rubric

	Excellent	Good	Fair	Poor	Self
Content— Complete The presentation included everything it should.	30 Presentation included all of the important information about the topic being presented.	20 Presentation covered most of the important information, but one key idea was missing.	10 Presentation covered some of the important information, but more than one key idea was missing.	0 Presentation included some information, but it was trivial or fluff.	
Content—Correct All of the information presented was accurate.	30 All of the information presented was accurate.	20 All of the information presented was correct with a few unintentional errors that were quickly corrected.	10 Most of the information presented was correct, but there were a few errors.	0 The information presented was not correct.	
Content— Consistency Speaker stayed on topic during the presentation.	10 Presenter stayed on topic 100% of the time.	7 Presenter stayed on topic 90–99% of the time.	4 Presenter stayed on topic 80–89% of the time.	0 It was hard to tell what the topic was.	
Prop Speaker had at least one prop that was directly related to the presentation.	20 Presenter had the prop and it complimented the presentation.	12 Presenter had a prop, but it was not the best choice.	4 Presenter had a prop, but there was no clear reason for its choice.	0 No prop.	
Flow Speaker knew the presentation well, so the words were well-spoken and flowed well together.	10 Presentation flowed well. Speaker did not stumble over words.	7 Some flow problems, but they did not distract from information.	4 Some flow problems interrupted presentation; presenter seemed flustered.	0 Constant flow problems; information was not presented in a way it could be understood.	
				Total Grade:	

Figure 4.3. Oral presentation rubric

Topic: _____ Student's Name_____

On a scale of 1–10, rate the following areas:

Content (Depth of information. How well did the speaker know his or her information? Was the information correct? Could the speaker answer questions?)	Your Ranking ▢	Give one specific reason why you gave this number.
Flow (Did the presentation flow smoothly? Did the speaker appear confident and ready to speak?)	Your Ranking ▢	Give one specific reason why you gave this number.
Prop (Did the speaker explain the prop he or she chose? Did the choice seem logical? Was it the best choice?)	Your Ranking ▢	Give one specific reason why you gave this number.

Comments: Below, write two specific things that you think the presenter did well.

- -

Topic: _____ Student's Name_____

On a scale of 1–10, rate the following areas:

Content (Depth of information. How well did the speaker know his or her information? Was the information correct? Could the speaker answer questions?)	Your Ranking ▢	Give one specific reason why you gave this number.
Flow (Did the presentation flow smoothly? Did the speaker appear confident and ready to speak?)	Your Ranking ▢	Give one specific reason why you gave this number.
Prop (Did the speaker explain the prop he or she chose? Did the choice seem logical? Was it the best choice?)	Your Ranking ▢	Give one specific reason why you gave this number.

Comments: Below, write two specific things that you think the presenter did well.

Figure 4.4. Student feedback rubric

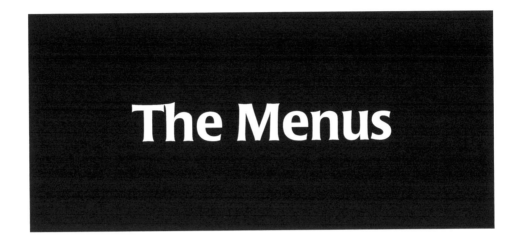

The Menus

How to Use the Menu Pages

Each menu in this section has:
- an introduction page for the teacher,
- the content menu,
- any specific guidelines, and
- activities mentioned in the menu.

Introduction Pages

The introduction pages are meant to provide an overview of each menu. They are divided into five areas.

1. *Objectives covered through the menu and activities.* This area will list all of the objectives that the menu can address. Menus are arranged in such a way that if students complete the guidelines set forth in the instructions for the menu, all of these objectives will be covered.

2. *Materials needed by students for completion.* For each menu, it is expected that the teacher will provide or students will have access to the following materials: lined paper; glue; crayons, colored pencils,

or markers; and blank 8 ½" by 11" white paper. The introduction page also includes a list of additional materials that may be needed by students. Students do have the choice about the menu items they can complete, so it is possible that the teacher will not need all of these materials for every student.

3. *Special notes.* Some menus allow students to choose to present demonstrations, songs, or PowerPoint presentations to their classmates. This section will give any special tips on managing these student presentations. This section will also share any tips to consider for a specific activity.

4. *Time frame.* Most menus are best used in at least a one-week time frame. Some are better suited to more than 2 weeks. This section will give you an overview about the best time frame for completing the entire menu, as well as options for shorter time periods. If teachers do not have time to devote to an entire menu, they can certainly choose the 1–2-day option for any menu topic students are currently studying.

5. *Suggested forms.* This is a list of the rubrics that should be available for students as the menus are introduced. If a menu has a free-choice option, the appropriate proposal form also will be listed here.

CHAPTER 5

Ancient History

Ancient Egypt

List Menu

Objectives Covered Through This Menu and These Activities
- Students will investigate the Egyptian number system.
- Students will describe the major events in Egyptian history.
- Students will investigate Egyptian pyramids and Egyptian culture.
- Students will explain mummification and its purpose.
- Students will look at the geography of Egypt and its impact on Egyptian life.

Materials Needed by Students for Completion
- Poster board or large white paper
- Graph paper or Internet access (for crossword puzzle)
- Materials for student created models (for Egyptian pyramid)
- Index cards (for recipe card)
- Video camera (for news report or commercial)
- Microsoft PowerPoint or other slideshow software
- Shoe boxes (for dioramas)
- Cube template
- Map of Egypt

Time Frame
- 1–2 weeks—Students are given the menu as the unit is started and the guidelines and point expectations are discussed. Because this menu covers one topic in depth, the teacher will go over all of the options on the menu and have students place checkmarks in the boxes next to the activities they are most interested in completing. As instruction continues, activities are completed by students and submitted for grading.
- 1–2 days—The teacher chooses an activity from an objective to use with the entire class during that lesson time.

Suggested Forms
- All-purpose rubric
- Proposal form for point-based projects
- $1 contract (for diorama)

Name:_____

Ancient Egypt Challenge Investigation

Guidelines:
1. You may complete as many of the activities listed as you would like within the time period given.
2. You may choose any combination of activities.
3. Your goal is 100 points. You may earn up to _____ points in extra credit.
4. You may be as creative as you like within the guidelines listed below.
5. You must show your plan to your teacher by _____.
6. Activities may be turned in at any time during the working time period. They will be graded and recorded on this sheet as you continue to work, so keep it safe!

Plan to Do	Activity to Complete	Point Value	Date Completed	Points Earned
	Investigate the Egyptian number system. Create and solve three math word problems using the Egyptian numbers.	25		
	Create a timeline for the major events in Egyptian history.	20		
	Create a PowerPoint presentation to share information about the Egyptian pyramids and how they were built.	20		
	The Egyptians used a written language called hieroglyphics. Research this language, and write a note to your friend in this code. Provide a key for the symbols that you used in your note.	25		
	Create a crossword puzzle about Ancient Egypt.	20		
	Make a model of an Egyptian pyramid.	20		
	Use a Venn diagram to compare the life of ancient Egyptians to American life today.	25		
	Choose an item of importance in ancient Egyptian life. Create a commercial to advertise the product.	25		
	Create a poster that shows the steps of mummification. Include the purpose behind the process and how mummification could be done today.	25		
	Complete the Egyptian Life Cube.	20		
	Write a story about the Nile River and its importance in Egyptian life.	20		
	Research the types of foods eaten by the Egyptians. Create a recipe card for a dish that may have been eaten at that time.	20		
	Write and perform a play about the life of a pharaoh as he prepares his pyramid.	25		
	Create a scale diorama of the pyramids of Giza.	20		
	Locate all of the Egyptian pyramids that have been found. Place these locations on a map.	15		
	A new pyramid has been discovered. Write a news story about its discovery and what the pyramid may contain.	30		
	Free choice: Must be outlined on a proposal form and approved before beginning work.			
	Total number of points you are planning to earn.		**Total points earned:**	

I am planning to complete _____ activities that could earn up to a total of _____ points.

Teacher's initials _____ Student's signature _____

Egyptian Life Cube

Complete the cube about Egyptian life. Use this pattern or create your own cube. Each side of the cube should be completed.

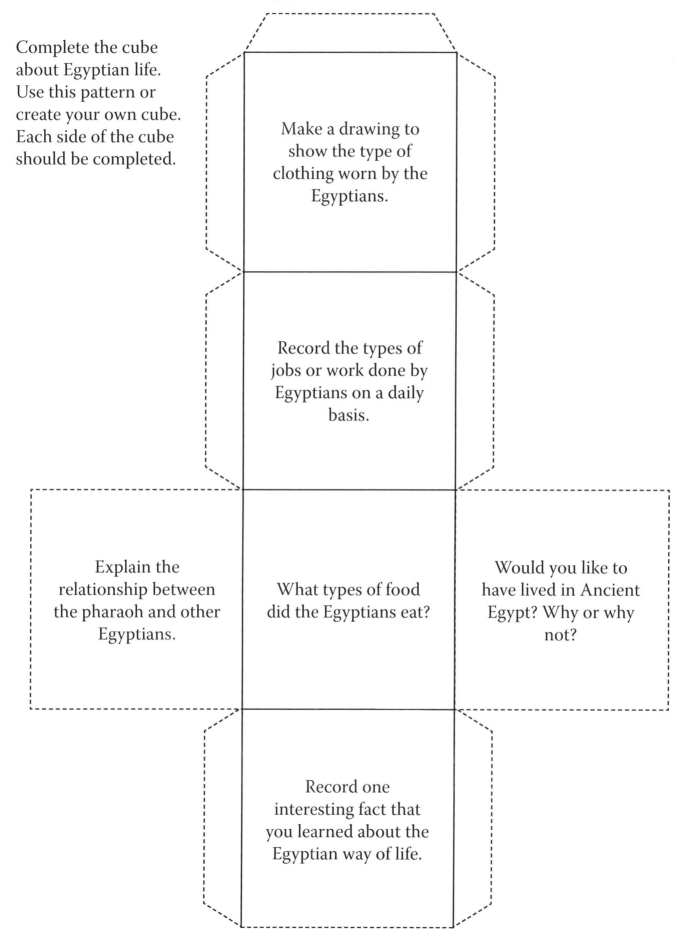

Make a drawing to show the type of clothing worn by the Egyptians.

Record the types of jobs or work done by Egyptians on a daily basis.

Explain the relationship between the pharaoh and other Egyptians.

What types of food did the Egyptians eat?

Would you like to have lived in Ancient Egypt? Why or why not?

Record one interesting fact that you learned about the Egyptian way of life.

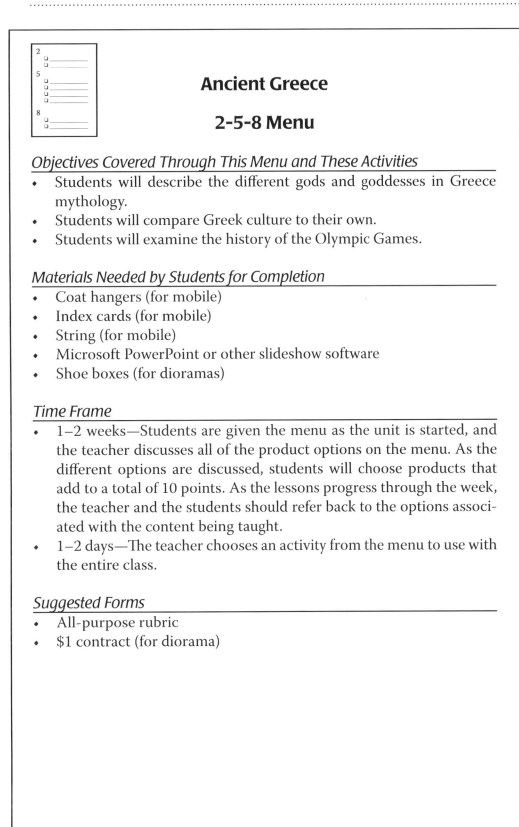

Ancient Greece

2-5-8 Menu

Objectives Covered Through This Menu and These Activities

- Students will describe the different gods and goddesses in Greece mythology.
- Students will compare Greek culture to their own.
- Students will examine the history of the Olympic Games.

Materials Needed by Students for Completion

- Coat hangers (for mobile)
- Index cards (for mobile)
- String (for mobile)
- Microsoft PowerPoint or other slideshow software
- Shoe boxes (for dioramas)

Time Frame

- 1–2 weeks—Students are given the menu as the unit is started, and the teacher discusses all of the product options on the menu. As the different options are discussed, students will choose products that add to a total of 10 points. As the lessons progress through the week, the teacher and the students should refer back to the options associated with the content being taught.
- 1–2 days—The teacher chooses an activity from the menu to use with the entire class.

Suggested Forms

- All-purpose rubric
- $1 contract (for diorama)

Name:_____

Ancient Greece

Directions: Choose two activities from the menu below. The activities must total 10 points. Place a checkmark in each box to show which activities you will complete. All activities must be completed by

_____.

---

2 Points

❏ The Greeks respected many gods. Create a mobile to show some of the gods and goddesses and their characteristics.

❏ Make a mind map to share information on Ancient Greece and its people.

---

5 Points

❏ Research the history of the Olympic games. Prepare a PowerPoint presentation to discuss their history and importance in Greece.

❏ Create a Venn diagram to compare and contrast the Olympic games of Greek times and modern day.

❏ Make an acrostic for three of the Greek gods or goddesses. For each letter of the gods' names, use words or phrases that describe his or her personality.

❏ Find a book that contains Greek myths. After reading one myth of your own choosing, make a diorama for the myth, and in your own words, retell it to your classmates.

---

8 Points

❏ Many myths have been written about the Greek gods. Develop your own myth about their latest adventure or problem.

❏ Great Greek philosophers created plays to tell the stories of the gods. Create your own play to tell a new story about Poseidon.

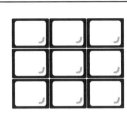

Ancient Rome

Game Show Menu

Objectives Covered Through This Menu and These Activities

- Students will examine the geography of Rome and its impact on Roman life.
- Students will look at the rise and fall of the Roman Empire.
- Students will explain how Latin has affected other romance languages.
- Students will compare the Roman societal structure with their own.
- Students will read and create myths.
- Students will investigate Roman numerals.
- Students will make connections between the Roman calendar and the calendar we use today.

Materials Needed by Students for Completion

- Materials for student-created lessons
- Magazines
- Coat hangers (for mobile)
- Index cards (for mobile)
- String (for mobile)
- Microsoft PowerPoint or other slideshow software
- Romulus and Remus legend (see The Legend of Romulus, Remus, and Rome)
- Calendar activity (see The Roman Calendar)

Time Frame

- 2–3 weeks—Students are given the menu as the unit is started and the guidelines and point expectations are discussed. As lessons are taught throughout the unit, students and the teacher can refer back to the options associated with that topic. The teacher will go over all of the options for the topic being covered and have students place checkmarks in the boxes next to the activities they are most interested in completing. As teaching continues over the next 2–3 weeks, activities are discussed, chosen, and submitted for grading.
- 1 week—At the start of the unit, the teacher chooses the three activities he or she feels are most valuable for the students. Stations can be set up in the classroom. These three activities are available for student choice throughout the week, as regular instruction takes place.

- 1–2 days—The teacher chooses an activity from the menu to use with the entire class.

Suggested Forms

- All-purpose rubric
- Oral report rubric
- Student-taught lesson rubric
- Proposal form for point-based projects

Guidelines for Ancient Rome Game Show Menu

- You must choose at least one activity from each topic area.
- You may not do more than two activities in any one topic area for credit. (You are, of course, welcome to do more than two for your own investigation.)
- Grading will be ongoing, so turn in products as you complete them.
- All free-choice proposals must be turned in and approved *prior* to working on that free choice.
- You must earn 120 points for a 100%. You may earn extra credit up to _____ points.
- You must show your teacher your plan for completion by: _____.

Ancient Rome

Geography	History	The Language	Society	The Myths	Numbers and Dates	Points for Each Level:
☐ Draw a map of the region that was Ancient Rome. (10 pts.)	☐ Create a timeline for the rise and fall of the Roman empire. (10 pts.)	☐ Research early Rome's language. Create a simple picture dictionary for 10 words. (15 pts.)	☐ Make a mobile to show the different Roman society groups and the privileges each had. (10 pts.)	☐ Read the myth of Romulus and Remus and illustrate the myth. (10 pts.)	☐ Make a chart that shows Roman numerals and how to use them to count. (10 pts.)	10–15 points
☐ Create a three-dimensional map of Ancient Rome. (20 pts.)	☐ The Roman army played an important role in the Roman Empire. Create a poster that shows its impact on Roman history. (20 pts.)	☐ Find examples of the Roman language in other languages spoken today. Create a PowerPoint presentation to share 10 words and their meanings. (25 pts.)	☐ Complete a Venn diagram to compare the lives of Plebeians and Patricians. (20 pts.)	☐ Choose your favorite Roman myth and adapt it into a play for your classmates. (25 pts.)	☐ Complete The Roman Calendar activity. (20 pts.)	20–25 points
☐ Create a lesson for your classmates to teach how the geography of Ancient Rome directly impacted the lives of the Romans. (30 pts.)	☐ Julius Caesar is one of the most famous Romans. You have discovered an awful plot against him. Write Julius a letter telling him everything you know and offering advice. (30 pts.)	☐ Latin is the basis for many modern languages, so why isn't it still spoken? Develop your own hypothesis and share your ideas through a PowerPoint presentation and speech. (30 pts.)	☐ Would you have been a good Roman? Prepare a speech that tells what qualities you possess that would have benefited you as a Roman citizen. (30 pts.)	☐ Write your own myth about the Roman god Mars. (30 pts.)	☐ Using Roman numerals and the Roman words for the months, write a creative story about a day in the life of a Roman child. (30 pts.)	30 points
Free Choice (prior approval) (25–50 pts.)	Free Choice (prior approval) (25–50 pts.)	Free Choice (prior approval) (25–50 pts.)	Free Choice (prior approval) (25–50 pts.)	Free Choice (prior approval) (25–50 pts.)	Free Choice (prior approval) (25–50 pts.)	25–50 points
Total:	Total:	Total:	Total:	Total:	Total:	Total Grade:

The Legend of Romulus, Remus, and Rome

Many tales and legends that explain the existence of ancient cities have been passed down throughout the ages. These legends are only as strong as the belief of the reader. This legend will tell one story of how Rome was built and by whom.

It would happen that Mars, the god of war, would fall in love with the priestess Rhea Silvia. This great love that he had for her led to her giving birth to twin boys, Romulus and Remus. Soon after their birth, a jealous family member cast them into the Tiber River. He hoped they would float away and drown, but he had not counted on the river waters falling and the boys floating ashore.

Once ashore, the boys were discovered by a she-wolf. Rather than killing the boys, she took pity on them, fed them, and looked after them. While with the wolf, the boys were discovered by Faustulus, a shepherd who brought the boys to his home for safe keeping. Faustulus and his wife decided to raise Romulus and Remus as their own children.

The boys grew up strong and clever and soon decided that they would like to leave their home. Although they thought about returning to their birthplace, they decided instead they would like to develop a city of their own. The boys chose the location along the Tiber River where they had been found and cared for by the she-wolf. The first step in designing the city was building the walls to define the land. Romulus took to the task, but Remus began to make fun of him. Remus said that the walls were too low to properly protect the city and he leaped over them to prove it. This greatly angered Romulus, and he killed his brother in rage. Romulus did not let this stop his efforts to create his own city. Romulus continued building his city and named it Roma—or Rome—after his own name. Although it was a new place, there were not many people who wished to move to this new city. Romulus now had his own city of outlaws and fugitives.

The Roman Calendar

The Roman calendar was a little different than our present-day calendar. Although it had 12 months, the year did not begin with January. Below are the names of all the months in the Roman order. Beside each, write the name we use for that month now.

_____ Martius—named for Mars, the god of war

_____ Aprilis—meaning "to open"

_____ Maius—named for Maia, the god of spring

_____ Junius—named for Juno, a Roman goddess

_____ Julius—named for Julius Caesar, the first Roman dictator

_____ Augustus—named for August Caesar, the first Roman emperor

_____ September—meaning 7

_____ October—meaning 8

_____ November—meaning 9

_____ December—meaning 10

_____ Januarius—named for Janus, the Roman god of gates

_____ Februarius—from *februare* (meaning "to clean")

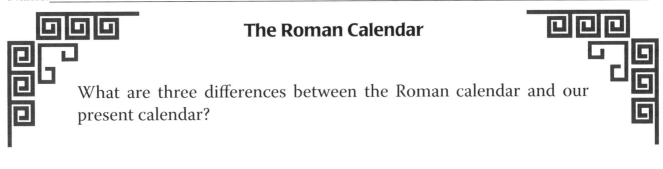

The Roman Calendar

What are three differences between the Roman calendar and our present calendar?

Think carefully about each of the names of the months; they were chosen for specific reasons. Below are six of the months. For each, explain why the Romans may have chosen that name for that time of year.

Aprilis

Maius

Augustus

September

Januarius

Februarius

CHAPTER 6

American History

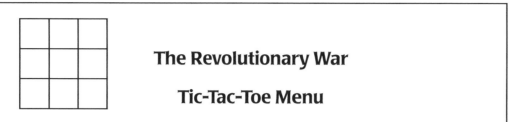

The Revolutionary War

Tic-Tac-Toe Menu

Objectives Covered Through This Menu and These Activities
- Students will examine the causes of the Revolutionary War.
- Students will analyze the results of the Revolutionary War on both the colonies and England.
- Students will show the major events of the Revolutionary War.

Materials Needed by Students for Completion
- Materials for three-dimensional timelines
- Materials for stacking model
- Video camera (for news report)
- Blank index cards (for trading cards)

Special Notes on the Use of This Menu
This menu gives the students the option to create a stacking model. This can be done in a number of different ways, such as stacking boxes with information written on them or having students stack their own three-dimensional shapes. The idea is to have students place the events in order as they "stacked up" to war being declared.

Time Frame
- 2 weeks—Students are given the menu as the unit is started. As the teacher presents lessons throughout the week, he or she should refer back to the options associated with that content. The teacher will go over all of the options for that content and have students place checkmarks in the boxes that represent the activities they are most interested in completing. As teaching continues over the next 2 weeks, activities chosen and completed should make a column or a row. When students make this pattern, they have completed one activity on the causes of the war, the results of the war, and the major events in the war.
- 1 week—At the start of the unit, the teacher chooses the three activities he or she feels are most valuable for the students. Stations can be set up in the classroom. These three activities are available for student choice throughout the week, as regular instruction takes place.
- 1–2 days—The teacher chooses an activity from the menu to use with the entire class.

Suggested Forms
- All-purpose rubric
- Oral report rubric
- Proposal form for projects

Name: _____

The Revolutionary War

☐ *Causes of the War* Create a set of trading cards for the events that led to the Revolutionary War.	☐ *Results of the War* Create a song or rap that describes how the colonies were changed after the war.	☐ *Major Events of the War* Pretend you are a person who just survived the most important event in the Revolutionary War. Write a journal entry describing your experience and why you felt it was the most significant.
☐ *Major Events of the War* Create a three-dimensional timeline that includes the significant events of the Revolutionary War.	☐ **Free Choice** (Fill out your proposal form before beginning the free choice!)	☐ *Results of the War* Create an advertisement to attract people to the colonies after the Revolutionary War. Why should they visit? How is it different?
☐ *Results of the War* Create a Venn diagram that compares the qualities of the colonies before and after the Revolutionary War.	☐ *Major Events of the War* You have been chosen to go to what could be the most important battle in the war—and it is taking place right now! Create a news report from the field describing what is happening, why it is happening, and why this could be a very important event.	☐ *Causes of the War* The war was caused by a series of events that built upon each other. Create a three-dimensional stacking model that shows the causes that led to the war.

Check the boxes you plan to complete. They should form a tic-tac-toe across or down.
All products are due by: _____.

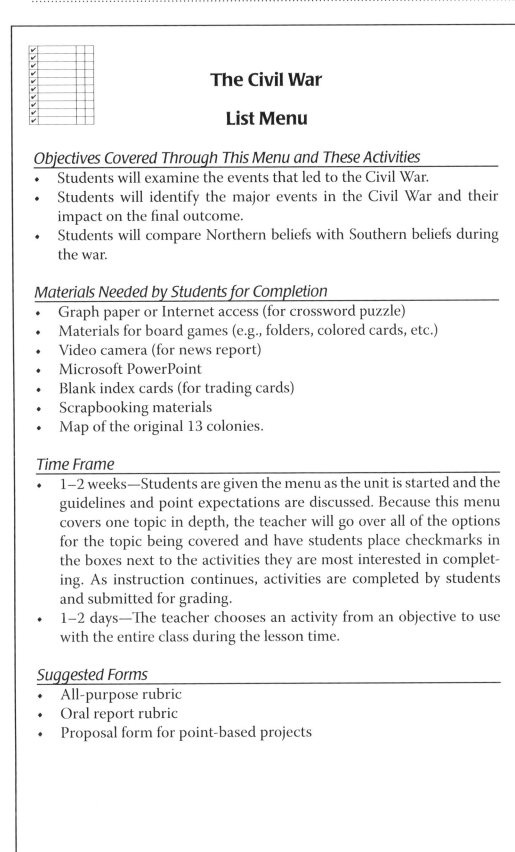

The Civil War

List Menu

Objectives Covered Through This Menu and These Activities

- Students will examine the events that led to the Civil War.
- Students will identify the major events in the Civil War and their impact on the final outcome.
- Students will compare Northern beliefs with Southern beliefs during the war.

Materials Needed by Students for Completion

- Graph paper or Internet access (for crossword puzzle)
- Materials for board games (e.g., folders, colored cards, etc.)
- Video camera (for news report)
- Microsoft PowerPoint
- Blank index cards (for trading cards)
- Scrapbooking materials
- Map of the original 13 colonies.

Time Frame

- 1–2 weeks—Students are given the menu as the unit is started and the guidelines and point expectations are discussed. Because this menu covers one topic in depth, the teacher will go over all of the options for the topic being covered and have students place checkmarks in the boxes next to the activities they are most interested in completing. As instruction continues, activities are completed by students and submitted for grading.
- 1–2 days—The teacher chooses an activity from an objective to use with the entire class during the lesson time.

Suggested Forms

- All-purpose rubric
- Oral report rubric
- Proposal form for point-based projects

Name:_____

The Civil War Challenge Investigation

Guidelines:
1. You may complete as many of the activities listed as you would like within the time period given.
2. You may choose any combination of activities.
3. Your goal is 100 points. You may earn up to _____ points in extra credit.
4. You may be as creative as you like within the guidelines listed below.
5. You must show your plan to your teacher by _____.
6. Activities may be turned in at any time during the working time period. They will be graded and recorded on this sheet as you continue to work, so keep it safe!

Plan to Do	Activity to Complete	Point Value	Date Completed	Points Earned
	Create a timeline of the events that led to the Civil War.	15		
	Make a book cover for an informational book about the Civil War.	20		
	Create a PowerPoint presentation comparing characteristics of the North and South before and after the Civil War.	25		
	Create a set of trading cards for the most important people who played a part in the Civil War.	20		
	Make a scrapbook with at least one page for a Northern soldier and one for a Southern soldier. Focus on the differences in their experiences.	25		
	Make a Civil War board game.	20		
	Make a crossword puzzle about the important events in the Civil War.	20		
	Choose the person you feel had the biggest impact in the war. Write a newspaper article about his or her impact and why you feel it was the most significant.	25		
	Using a map of the original 13 states, mark the location of the major battles in the Civil War.	10		
	You have been asked to cover the surrender of General Lee at Appomattox Courthouse. Create a news report to document the event.	25		
	Many families were split by the Civil War. Pretend you are a Southern soldier writing to your Northern family. Explain your choice in fighting for the South.	25		
	There were many songs from the Civil War time period. Research them and perform one for your classmates.	20		
	Create a song that tells the tale of the Civil War.	25		
	Free choice: Must be outlined on a proposal form and approved before beginning work.			
	Total number of points you are planning to earn.		**Total points earned:**	

I am planning to complete _____ activities that could earn up to a total of _____ points.

Teacher's initials _____ Student's signature _____

Mustang Flats

2-5-8 Menu

This lesson revolves around the novel *Mustang Flats*, by G. Clifton Wisler. This story takes place in Texas. Alby has been left to care for his family and the family farm when his father goes to fight in the Civil War. There are many sacrifices that have to be made in order to keep the family together. After the war ends, his father returns—a man he doesn't seem to know anymore. The family farm is now in poor condition due to the Confederate dollars losing their value. Desperate for money, the family decides to capture and break wild mustangs to pay for their necessities.

Objectives Covered Through This Menu and These Activities
- Students will examine the battles fought in the Civil War.
- Students will analyze the impact of the Civil War on families left behind.
- Students will experience the effects of the Civil War on a southern family.

Materials Needed by Students for Completion
- *Mustang Flats* by G. Clifton Wisler (Puffin)
- Poster board or large white paper
- Video camera (for news report)
- Story map for fiction

Time Frame
- 1–2 weeks—Students are given the menu as the unit is started, and the teacher discusses all of the product options on the menu. As the different options are discussed, students will choose products that add to a total of 10 points. As the lessons progress through the week, the teacher and the students should refer back to the options associated with the content being taught.
- 1–2 days—The teacher chooses an activity from the menu to use with the entire class.

Suggested Forms
- All-purpose rubric

Mustang Flats

Directions: Choose two activities from the menu below. The activities must total 10 points. Place a checkmark in each box to show which activities you will complete. All activities must be completed by _____.

2 Points

- ❑ Research the battles that Nebo and Alby's father discuss. Make a flipbook that shows the location of the battles and the outcome.

- ❑ Complete a story map for *Mustang Flats.*

5 Points

- ❑ Make a Venn diagram that compares Alby's life before and after the war.

- ❑ There were only so many ways a family could make money after the Confederate dollars lost their value. Make a poster that shows the ways that Alby's family tried to make money, as well as other ideas of your own that you think would be helpful.

- ❑ The family never gave up hope that Pa would return. Create a news report that documents his journey and his feelings about arriving at home.

- ❑ Free choice—Prepare a proposal form and submit it to your teacher for approval.

8 Points

- ❑ Pa made an interesting decision about the wild stallion called Demon. Think about why he made that decision. Write a journal entry that Pa might have written telling his thoughts on this matter.

- ❑ Uncle Mitch tells Alby that usually the worst injuries to a man who has gone to war are the ones inside. Look through *Mustang Flats* and find examples and quotes from the text that prove Uncle Mitch correct. Write a report that shares all of the examples you have located and explains the meaning behind Uncle Mitch's words.

Story Map

Title and Author	Setting

Main Characters
With At Least Three Traits for Each

Supporting Characters
With One Sentence About Why They Are Important

Problem

Major Events in the Story

Solution

© Prufrock Press Inc. • *Differentiating Instruction With Menus: Social Studies* • *Grades 3–5*

This page may be photocopied or reproduced with permission for student use.

57

Westward Expansion

2-5-8 Menu

Objectives Covered Through This Menu and These Activities
- Students will explain the reasons why people chose to travel west.
- Students will understand what kinds of hardships and adventures settlers may have encountered on their journey.

Materials Needed by Students for Completion
- Materials for board games (e.g., folders, colored cards, etc.)
- Video camera (for news report)
- Shoe boxes (for dioramas)

Time Frame
- 1–2 weeks—Students are given the menu as the unit is started, and the teacher discusses all of the product options on the menu. As the different options are discussed, students will choose products that add to a total of 10 points. As the lessons progress through the week, the teacher and the students should refer back to the options associated with the content being taught.
- 1–2 days—The teacher chooses an activity from the menu to use with the entire class.

Suggested Forms
- All-purpose rubric

Name:_____

Westward Expansion

Directions: Choose two activities from the menu below. The activities must total 10 points. Place a checkmark in each box to show which activities you will complete. All activities must be completed by

_____.

---

2 Points

❏ Make a windowpane to explain Westward expansion and show the reasons why Westward expansion took place.

❏ Create a diorama that shows a scene you may have seen during the trips taken by settlers moving West.

---

5 Points

❏ When people traveled in large groups, they often came up with songs to pass the time during the trip West. Create your own song about the trip that could have been sung around the campfire at night.

❏ Create a Westward expansion board game. Be as realistic as possible in its design.

❏ Although television had not been invented during this time period, create a news report to share the information about this movement. Why are people moving? What do they hope to gain? Should everyone go?

❏ Create an advertising brochure for a company helping settlers move West. What should they include to entice settlers to use their company?

---

8 Points

❏ You are traveling Westward. Write five journal entries that explain your reasons for taking the trip, and the adventures or misfortunes you encounter on the trip.

❏ Your family has decided to travel Westward. Create a play that shows why you decided to move, what you hope to accomplish, and what happens along the way.

Industrial Revolution

2-5-8 Menu

Objectives Covered Through This Menu and These Activities

- Students will explain the Industrial Revolution.
- Students will explain the effects of the Industrial Revolution on the United States.
- Students will show some of the major inventions that resulted from the Industrial Revolution.

Materials Needed by Students for Completion

- Graph paper or Internet access (for crossword puzzle)
- Magazines (for collage)
- Video camera (for news report)
- Coat hangers (for mobile)
- Index cards (for mobile)
- String (for mobile)
- Microsoft PowerPoint or other slideshow software
- Cube template
- Ruler (for comic strip)

Time Frame

- 1–2 weeks—Students are given the menu as the unit is started, and the teacher discusses all of the product options on the menu. As the different options are discussed, students will choose products that add to a total of 10 points. As the lessons progress through the week, the teacher and the students should refer back to the options associated with the content being taught.
- 1–2 days—The teacher chooses an activity from the menu to use with the entire class.

Suggested Forms

- All-purpose rubric

Name:_____

Industrial Revolution

Directions: Choose two activities from the menu below. The activities must total 10 points. Place a checkmark in each box to show which activities you will complete. All activities must be completed by _____.

---

2 Points

❑ Create a mobile about the Industrial Revolution with at least eight examples of developments that took place during this time period.

❑ Make a quiz to give your classmates about the events that occurred during the Industrial Revolution.

---

5 Points

❑ Create a comic strip that shows how the Industrial Revolution changed the lives of Americans.

❑ Create a crossword puzzle about the Industrial Revolution.

❑ Complete a cube with six different inventions that were developed during the Industrial Revolution.

❑ Prepare a news report about the new wave of industry that seems to be sweeping the country.

---

8 Points

❑ Choose the most important development or invention, in your opinion, from the Industrial Revolution. Create a PowerPoint presentation that shares the development, how it was created, and its impact on the future.

❑ The Industrial Revolution changed history in many ways. Pretend you are living through these great changes. Write a story about your experiences and how the revolution is changing your life.

Industrial Revolution Invention Cube

Complete the cube about inventions developed during the Industrial Revolution. Each side of the cube should include one invention developed, a description of the invention, and a drawing or photo if possible. Use this pattern or create your own cube.

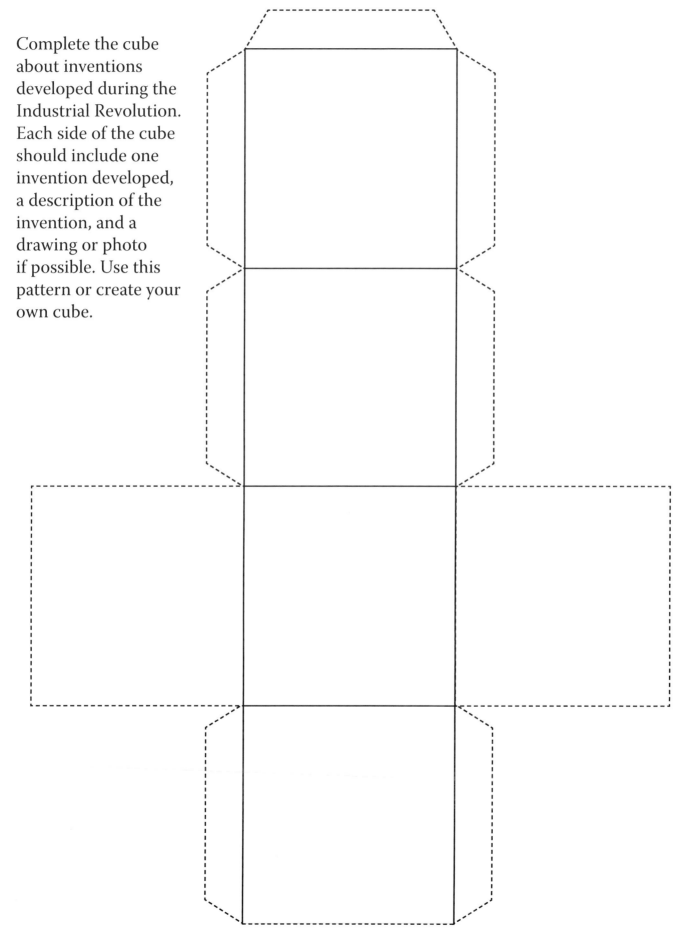

Lyddie

List Menu

This lesson revolves around the novel *Lyddie*, by Katherine Paterson. In this novel, Lyddie learns firsthand the importance of hard work. After her family loses its farm to debt, she strives to make enough money to pay off the debt and regain the farm. Her quest begins when she is put into service by her mother at an inn. Eventually, Lyddie leaves the inn to work for a mill that makes cloth on large and noisy looms. Although Lyddie can neither read nor write well when she gets the job at the mill, she works extremely long hours in hard conditions. She uses her time creatively to learn to read and write by reading *Oliver Twist* while tending her looms. Lyddie makes a lot of money by working these long hours and hopes to pay off her family farm. There are people in the mill, however, who want to pass a petition for better working conditions. Lyddie has to decide if she wants to sign such a petition when money is so important to her.

Objectives Covered Through This Menu and These Activities
- Students will examine the working conditions in the mills during the Industrial Revolution.
- Students will compare the quality of life during this time period with their own.
- Students will understand how the Industrial Revolution changed many lives.
- Students will understand the movement for better working conditions.

Materials Needed by Students for Completion
- *Lyddie* by Katherine Paterson (Puffin)
- *Oliver Twist* by Charles Dickens
- Poster board or large white paper
- Materials for student-created product (their choice to compare with *Oliver Twist*)
- Microsoft PowerPoint or other slideshow software
- Materials for student-created models (for loom)

Special Notes on the Use of This Menu
There are two scenes in this book that may make it inappropriate for your grade level or students. First, Lyddie defends one of her female coworkers against the inappropriate advances of her boss. The book does not go

into a lot of detail, but it does lead to Lyddie being fired. Secondly, Diana, the activist, does get pregnant out of wedlock and needs to leave the mill. The book is not detailed in its description of this situation; it states it and moves quickly on. Taking into account your students and their backgrounds, either of these situations could be inappropriate.

Time Frame

- 1–2 weeks—Students are given the menu as the unit is started and the guidelines and point expectations on the back of the menu are discussed. Because this menu covers one topic in depth, the teacher will go over all the options for the topic being covered and have students place checkmarks in the boxes next to the activities they are most interested in completing. As instruction continues, activities are completed by students and submitted for grading.
- 1–2 days—The teacher chooses an activity from an objective to use with the entire class during that lesson time.

Suggested Forms

- All-purpose rubric
- Oral report rubric
- Proposal form for point-based projects

Name:_____

Lyddie **Challenge Investigation**

Guidelines:

1. You may complete as many of the activities listed as you would like within the time period given.
2. You may choose any combination of activities.
3. Your goal is 100 points. You may earn up to _____ points in extra credit.
4. You may be as creative as you like within the guidelines listed below.
5. You must show your plan to your teacher by _____.
6. Activities may be turned in at any time during the working time period. They will be graded and recorded on this sheet as you continue to work, so keep it safe!

Plan to Do	Activity to Complete	Point Value	Date Completed	Points Earned
	Make a Venn diagram to compare working conditions in the mill with working conditions now.	20		
	Many girls wanted to come and work in the mills. Write a letter from one of these girls to her family explaining why she wants to work there.	20		
	Make a model of a loom.	15		
	Acting as a newspaper reporter, interview Diana about her cause. Write a newspaper article explaining her point of view.	30		
	The mill owners often spoke against the petitions for workers' rights. Prepare a speech to explain why, as a mill owner, you do not agree with their petition.	25		
	Create a PowerPoint presentation that shows how the Industrial Revolution changed the lives of farmers. Use examples from the story to support your ideas.	20		
	Research the school that Lyddie and Betsy wanted to attend in Ohio. Create an advertisement to draw more women to the school.	20		
	This time period was quite different from our lives now. Determine at least 20 differences between Lyddie's life and yours. Create a poster to show these differences.	25		
	Lyddie really loved the book *Oliver Twist*. Compare her life with that of Oliver. Create a product to show this comparison.	30		
	Free choice: Must be outlined on a proposal form and approved before beginning work.			
	Total number of points you are planning to earn.		**Total points earned:**	

I am planning to complete _____ activities that could earn up to a total of _____ points.

Teacher's initials _____ Student's signature _____

Our State's History

2-5-8 Menu

Objectives Covered Through This Menu and These Activities

- Students will identify important events in their state's history.
- Students will locate on a map their state's historical locations.
- Students will understand the significance of their state's historical locations.
- Students will choose the leader who has had the greatest impact on their state's history.

Materials Needed by Students for Completion

- Graph paper or Internet access (for crossword puzzle)
- Microsoft PowerPoint or other slideshow software
- Materials for three-dimensional timelines

Time Frame

- 1–2 weeks—Students are given the menu as the unit is started, and the teacher discusses all of the product options on the menu. As the different options are discussed, students will choose products that add to a total of 10 points. As the lessons progress through the week, the teacher and the students should refer back to the options associated with the content being taught.
- 1–2 days—The teacher chooses an activity from the menu to use with the entire class.

Suggested Forms

- All-purpose rubric
- Oral report rubric

Name:_____

Our State's History

Directions: Choose two activities from the menu below. The activities must total 10 points. Place a checkmark in each box to show which activities you will complete. All activities must be completed by _____.

---

2 Points

❒ Make a flipbook of the important events in our state's history.

❒ Create a crossword puzzle about our state's history.

---

5 Points

❒ Create a three-dimensional timeline of the 10 most significant events in our state's history.

❒ Design an advertisement for one of our state's historical locations.

❒ Design a book cover for a book about our state's history.

❒ Create a board game based on our state.

---

8 Points

❒ Choose one of our state's great leaders who you feel made the biggest difference in where we are today. Come to school as this person to talk about your impact on our state.

❒ Which of our state's historic sites do you think is most important to other students your age? Create a PowerPoint presentation that gives information about the site, as well as why it is the most important to you.

CHAPTER 7

Government

Our Government

Tic-Tac-Toe Menu

Objectives Covered Through This Menu and These Activities
- Students will identify the three branches of our government.
- Students will explain the purposes our government serves.
- Students will examine the different public offices of our government and their duties.

Materials Needed by Students for Completion
- Poster board or large white paper
- Coat hangers (for mobile)
- Index cards (for mobile)
- String (for mobile)
- Blank index cards (for trading cards)
- Cube template

Time Frame
- 2 weeks—Students are given the menu as the unit is started. As the teacher presents lessons throughout the week, he or she should refer back to the options associated with that content. The teacher will go over all of the options for that content and have students place checkmarks in the boxes that represent the activities they are most interested in completing. As teaching continues over the next 2 weeks, activities chosen and completed should make a column or a row. When students make this pattern, they have completed one activity on the three branches of government, the purposes of government, and the duties and roles of our public offices.
- 1 week—At the start of the unit, the teacher chooses the three activities he or she feels are most valuable for the students. Stations can be set up in the classroom. These three activities are available for student choice throughout the week, as regular instruction takes place.
- 1–2 days—The teacher chooses an activity from the menu to use with the entire class.

Suggested Forms
- All-purpose rubric
- Oral report rubric
- Proposal form for projects

Name:_____

Our Government

☐ **The Three Branches** Create a mobile for the three branches of the government. Include the responsibilities of each branch.	☐ **Public Offices** Create a set of trading cards for the different public offices that can be held in our state. Include the duties and qualities of the person who should hold that office.	☐ **Purposes of Government** The U.S. Government serves an important role in the daily life of Americans. Prepare a speech that explains how the actions of the government affect your daily life.
☐ **Public Offices** You are running for a local public office. Which office would you choose? Create a campaign poster to help you get that position. Include the qualities you possess that make you a good candidate for the position.	☐ **Free Choice** (Fill out your proposal form before beginning the free choice!)	☐ **The Three Branches** Create a flipbook for the three branches of government. Include the responsibilities for each branch on the pages.
☐ **Purposes of Government** Complete the government cube and outline the purposes of the government.	☐ **The Three Branches** Create a pamphlet to teach other students your age about the branches of government and what they do to help us.	☐ **Public Offices** As a newspaper writer, you often have to interview public people. Develop an interview that you would use to interview one of your public officials to learn more about his or her job. Then interview the person and write the article.

Check the boxes you plan to complete. They should form a tic-tac-toe across or down. All products are due by: _____.

The Purpose of Our Government Cube

Complete the cube about our government. Each side of the cube should include one purpose or role that the government serves for its people. Each role should be described and examples should be given. Use this pattern or create your own cube.

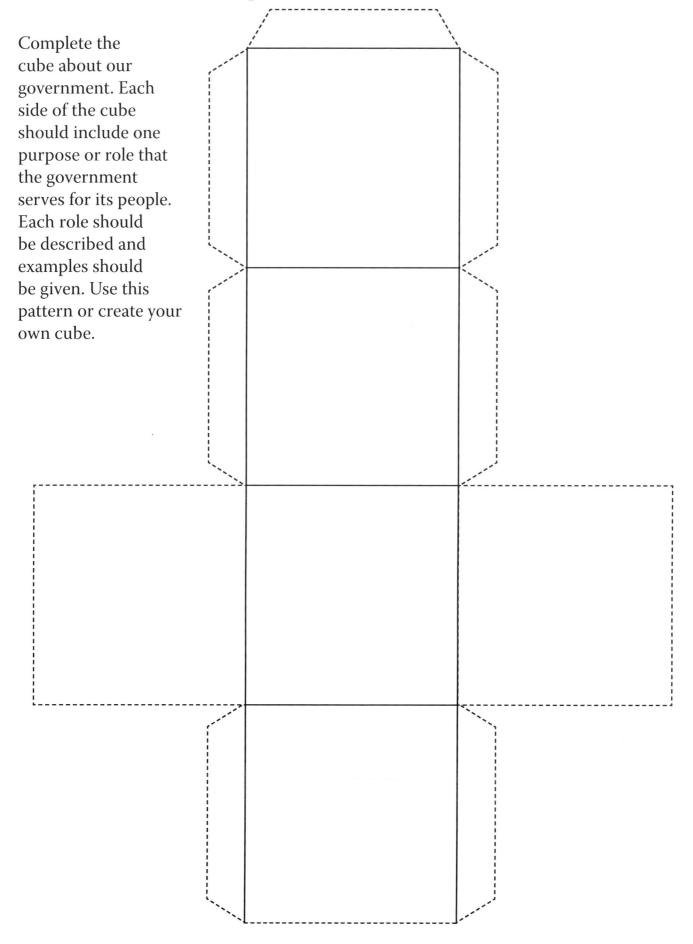

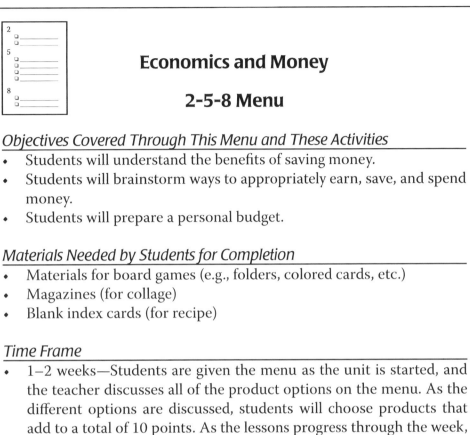

Economics and Money

2-5-8 Menu

Objectives Covered Through This Menu and These Activities

- Students will understand the benefits of saving money.
- Students will brainstorm ways to appropriately earn, save, and spend money.
- Students will prepare a personal budget.

Materials Needed by Students for Completion

- Materials for board games (e.g., folders, colored cards, etc.)
- Magazines (for collage)
- Blank index cards (for recipe)

Time Frame

- 1–2 weeks—Students are given the menu as the unit is started, and the teacher discusses all of the product options on the menu. As the different options are discussed, students will choose products that add to a total of 10 points. As the lessons progress through the week, the teacher and the students should refer back to the options associated with the content being taught.
- 1–2 days—The teacher chooses an activity from the menu to use with the entire class.

Suggested Forms

- All-purpose rubric

Name:_____

Economics and Money

Directions: Choose two activities from the menu below. The activities must total 10 points. Place a checkmark in each box to show which activities you will complete. All activities must be completed by _____.

---

2 Points

❑ Create an acrostic for the words *save* and *earn*. For each, record ways to do both of these.

❑ Create a recipe card for a successful budget including the key ingredients for success.

---

5 Points

❑ Create a collage of items that you would buy if you had $1,000. Include the price by each item so it is clear that you did not exceed your budget.

❑ Create a song that tells about ways that you and your classmates could earn and save money.

❑ Design an advertisement to get others your age to start saving money. Include information about why saving is important and what items they may want to save for in the future.

❑ Create a money board game in which players spend, budget, and save money.

---

8 Points

❑ Create a budget that you could use for 2 weeks to save money. Record your plan, share it with your parents, and put it into effect for 2 weeks. At the end of 2 weeks, evaluate your plan's success and make recommendations to make it better. Develop a report that includes your plan, your records, your evaluation, and suggestions.

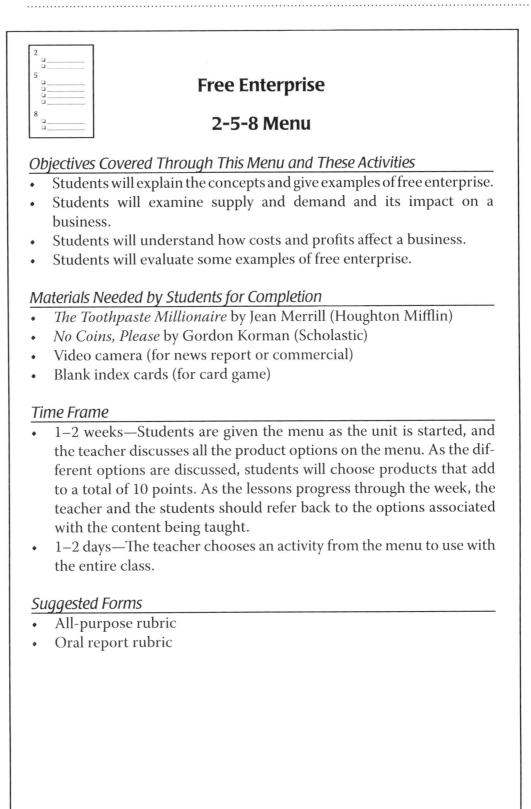

Free Enterprise

2-5-8 Menu

Objectives Covered Through This Menu and These Activities

- Students will explain the concepts and give examples of free enterprise.
- Students will examine supply and demand and its impact on a business.
- Students will understand how costs and profits affect a business.
- Students will evaluate some examples of free enterprise.

Materials Needed by Students for Completion

- *The Toothpaste Millionaire* by Jean Merrill (Houghton Mifflin)
- *No Coins, Please* by Gordon Korman (Scholastic)
- Video camera (for news report or commercial)
- Blank index cards (for card game)

Time Frame

- 1–2 weeks—Students are given the menu as the unit is started, and the teacher discusses all the product options on the menu. As the different options are discussed, students will choose products that add to a total of 10 points. As the lessons progress through the week, the teacher and the students should refer back to the options associated with the content being taught.
- 1–2 days—The teacher chooses an activity from the menu to use with the entire class.

Suggested Forms

- All-purpose rubric
- Oral report rubric

Free Enterprise

Directions: Choose two activities from the menu below. The activities must total 10 points. Place a checkmark in each box to show which activities you will complete. All activities must be completed by _____.

2 Points

❑ Make an acrostic for the words *free enterprise*. Place a word or phrase for each letter that explains free enterprise or gives examples.

❑ Make a concentration game for the important words and definitions about free enterprise.

5 Points

❑ You are a news reporter who will be reporting on a local supply and demand issue and how it is affecting costs of the product. Choose your issue and create a news report to share the information.

❑ Make a brochure that explains how to run a successful simple business. Include information and examples on cost and profits, supply and demand, and other important considerations.

❑ It can be a big decision to start a small business. Prepare a commercial for a company that helps other people start their own small business. Include all the important information about a small business, as well as why people would want to use your company to start their own.

8 Points

❑ Read either *The Toothpaste Millionaire* or *No Coins, Please*. Both of these books are about children taking advantage of free enterprise. Create your own idea for free enterprise. Make a Venn diagram to compare the plan for your idea with the plan you read about in the book you chose.

❑ Develop your own idea for a simple business. Create a business plan that addresses the key ideas of cost versus profit and supply and demand. Present your idea to your teacher and put your plan into action.

CHAPTER 8

U.S. Documents

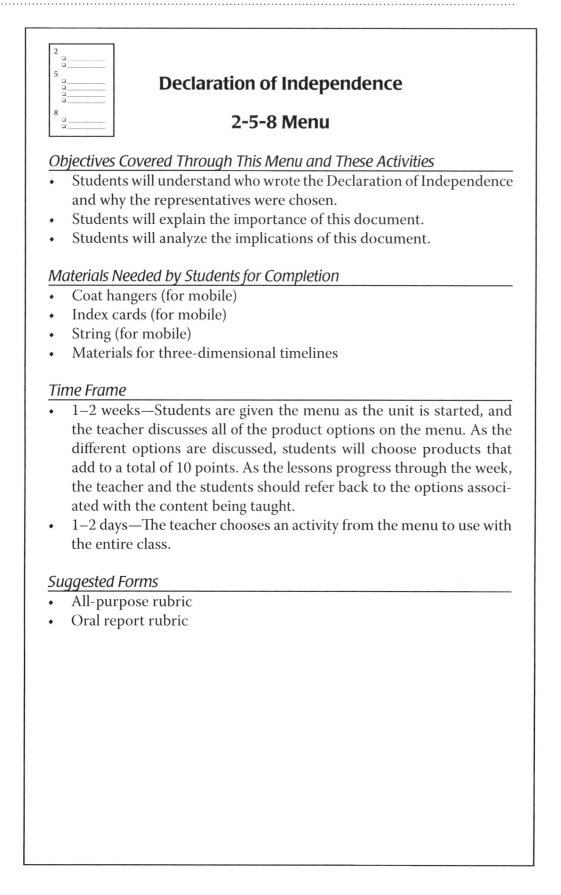

Declaration of Independence

2-5-8 Menu

Objectives Covered Through This Menu and These Activities
- Students will understand who wrote the Declaration of Independence and why the representatives were chosen.
- Students will explain the importance of this document.
- Students will analyze the implications of this document.

Materials Needed by Students for Completion
- Coat hangers (for mobile)
- Index cards (for mobile)
- String (for mobile)
- Materials for three-dimensional timelines

Time Frame
- 1–2 weeks—Students are given the menu as the unit is started, and the teacher discusses all of the product options on the menu. As the different options are discussed, students will choose products that add to a total of 10 points. As the lessons progress through the week, the teacher and the students should refer back to the options associated with the content being taught.
- 1–2 days—The teacher chooses an activity from the menu to use with the entire class.

Suggested Forms
- All-purpose rubric
- Oral report rubric

Name:_____

Declaration of Independence

Directions: Choose two activities from the menu below. The activities must total 10 points. Place a checkmark in each box to show which activities you will complete. All activities must be completed by _____.

---

2 Points

❏ Record the names of all the people who signed the Declaration of Independence, the state they represented, and their position in that state.

❏ Make a mobile that shows the ideas expressed in the Declaration of Independence.

---

5 Points

❏ Create a three-dimensional timeline that begins on June 7, 1776, and shows the chronology of events for the Declaration of Independence, from the first idea to its publication for every state by Mary Katherine Goddard.

❏ You have been asked to represent your state and sign the newly developed Declaration of Independence but you are not sure you should. What reasons might you have for not signing this new document? Write an editorial for the newspaper to explain why someone may not want to sign this document.

❏ Look at each section of the Declaration of Independence. Create a windowpane to discuss the purpose of each section.

❏ The Declaration of Independence is titled: "The unanimous Declaration of the thirteen united States of America." These words were carefully chosen for their meaning. Create a speech about what this simple yet meaningful statement means.

---

8 Points

❏ Has there ever been an occasion when you wanted to declare independence from someone or something? Think about why you wanted to do this and outline your own Declaration of Independence for the situation. Follow the same format as the Declaration of Independence of 1776.

❏ Write and, with the help of your classmates, perform a play about the designing and signing of the Declaration of Independence and its implications for the original 13 United States.

The Bill of Rights

2-5-8 Menu

Objectives Covered Through This Menu and These Activities

- Students will describe the rights outlined in this document and their importance in our daily lives.
- Students will give examples of the different rights in this document.

Materials Needed by Students for Completion

- Materials for board games (e.g., folders, colored cards, etc.)
- Coat hangers (mobile)
- Index cards (mobile)
- String (mobile)
- Cube template

Time Frame

- 1–2 weeks—Students are given the menu as the unit is started, and the teacher discusses all of the product options on the menu. As the different options are discussed, students will choose products that add to a total of 10 points. As the lessons progress through the week, the teacher and the students should refer back to the options associated with the content being taught.
- 1–2 days—The teacher chooses an activity from the menu to use with the entire class.

Suggested Forms

- All-purpose rubric
- Oral report rubric

The Bill of Rights

Directions: Choose two activities from the menu below. The activities must total 10 points. Place a checkmark in each box to show which activities you will complete. All activities must be completed by
_____.

---

2 Points

❑ Complete the Bill of Rights cube. On each side, write one amendment, summarize it, and give an example of the right this amendment grants.

❑ Make a Bill of Rights mobile in which you include the basic rights, what they state, and an example for each.

---

5 Points

❑ Although the Bill of Rights is a document, if it were made into a book, it would need a book cover. Design one for the *Book of Rights*.

❑ Create a brochure about the importance of the Bill of Rights.

❑ Create a board game that has a Bill of Rights theme.

❑ As a newspaper writer, you have been asked to interview the person in charge of developing the Bill of Rights. Develop a set of questions you would like to have answered, and create realistic answers.

---

8 Points

❑ Prepare and give a speech that shares which right is the most important to you and why you feel this way. Provide examples to persuade your audience.

❑ Imagine how our country would be different if the Bill of Rights had not been written. Write a story that tells what the United States would be like today if that were the case.

Bill of Rights Cube

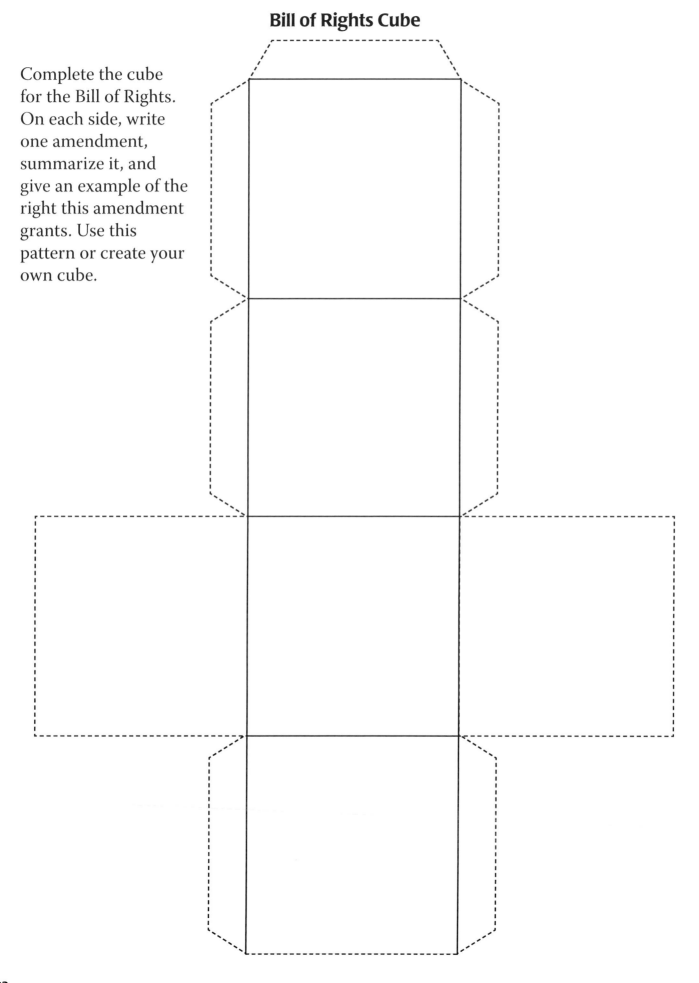

Complete the cube for the Bill of Rights. On each side, write one amendment, summarize it, and give an example of the right this amendment grants. Use this pattern or create your own cube.

The Constitution

Tic-Tac-Toe Menu

Objectives Covered Through This Menu and These Activities

- Students will explain the importance of the amendments to the Constitution.
- Students will examine the history of the Constitution's development.
- Students will evaluate the guarantees found in the Constitution.

Materials Needed by Students for Completion

- Video camera (for news report)
- Coat hangers (for mobile)
- Index cards (for mobile)
- String (for mobile)
- Microsoft PowerPoint or other slideshow software

Time Frame

- 2 weeks—Students are given the menu as the unit is started. As the teacher presents lessons throughout the week, he or she should refer back to the options associated with that content. The teacher will go over all of the options for that content and have students place checkmarks in the boxes that represent the activities they are most interested in completing. As teaching continues over the next 2 weeks, activities chosen and completed should make a column or a row. When students make this pattern, they have completed one activity on the history of the Constitution, the Amendments, and the guarantees the Constitution provides.
- 1 week—At the start of the unit, the teacher chooses the three activities he or she feels are most valuable for the students. Stations can be set up in the classroom. These three activities are available for student choice throughout the week, as regular instruction takes place.
- 1–2 days—The teacher chooses an activity from the menu to use with the entire class.

Suggested Forms:

- All-purpose rubric
- Oral report rubric
- Proposal form for projects

The Constitution

☐ **History of the Constitution** Create a timeline that shows the major events that led to the signing of the Constitution.	☐ **The Amendments** Prepare a speech about the amendment that you feel is most important. Your speech should share examples of the guaranteed rights and why you feel the amendment is most important.	☐ **Guarantees of the Constitution** The Constitution was quite different from the Articles of Confederacy. Make a Venn diagram to compare and contrast the two documents.
☐ **The Amendments** Create a worksheet to quiz your classmates about their knowledge of the amendments to the Constitution. Use basic questions, as well as real-life examples, of the rights and freedoms.	☐ **Free Choice** (Fill out your proposal form before beginning the free choice!)	☐ **History of the Constitution** Write a play that documents the long days of debate when the delegates gathered in Philadelphia to discuss the effectiveness of the Articles of Confederacy.
☐ **Guarantees of the Constitution** Create a mobile that shows the seven articles of the Constitution. Include what the article stated and information about each.	☐ **History of the Constitution** Many delegates attended the meeting in Philadelphia. Create a news report about the development of the Constitution by interviewing the person you feel had the greatest impact on its outcome.	☐ **The Amendments** Create a PowerPoint presentation that shows the rights and freedoms expressed in the amendments to the Constitution.

Check the boxes you plan to complete. They should form a tic-tac-toe across or down.

All products are due by: _____.

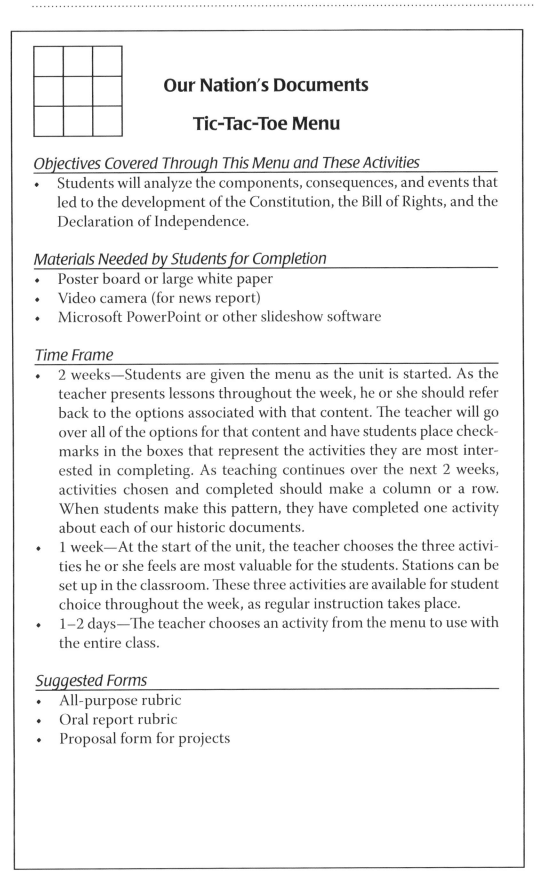

Our Nation's Documents

Tic-Tac-Toe Menu

Objectives Covered Through This Menu and These Activities

- Students will analyze the components, consequences, and events that led to the development of the Constitution, the Bill of Rights, and the Declaration of Independence.

Materials Needed by Students for Completion

- Poster board or large white paper
- Video camera (for news report)
- Microsoft PowerPoint or other slideshow software

Time Frame

- 2 weeks—Students are given the menu as the unit is started. As the teacher presents lessons throughout the week, he or she should refer back to the options associated with that content. The teacher will go over all of the options for that content and have students place checkmarks in the boxes that represent the activities they are most interested in completing. As teaching continues over the next 2 weeks, activities chosen and completed should make a column or a row. When students make this pattern, they have completed one activity about each of our historic documents.
- 1 week—At the start of the unit, the teacher chooses the three activities he or she feels are most valuable for the students. Stations can be set up in the classroom. These three activities are available for student choice throughout the week, as regular instruction takes place.
- 1–2 days—The teacher chooses an activity from the menu to use with the entire class.

Suggested Forms

- All-purpose rubric
- Oral report rubric
- Proposal form for projects

Our Nation's Documents

The Constitution Create a timeline that shows the major events that led to the signing of the Constitution.	**Bill of Rights** Prepare a speech about the amendment you feel is most important. Your speech will share examples of the rights it protects and why you feel it is the most important.	**Declaration of Independence** Create an informational brochure about the Declaration of Independence. Discuss its development and impact on the United States.
Bill of Rights Design an activity or lesson for your classmates about the Bill of Rights and what it means to Americans.	**Free Choice** (Fill out your proposal form before beginning the free choice!)	**The Constitution** Many delegates attended the meeting in Philadelphia. With a partner, create a news report about the development of the Constitution, interviewing the person you feel had the greatest impact on its outcome.
Declaration of Independence Write a play that shows the major events that occurred between July 4, 1776, and January 17, 1777.	**The Constitution** After reading the Constitution, choose one phrase that meant the most to you. Design a poster around that quote showing why that phrase is so meaningful.	**Bill of Rights** Create a PowerPoint presentation that shows the rights and freedoms expressed in the Amendments to the Constitution.

Check the boxes you plan to complete. They should form a tic-tac-toe across or down.
All products are due by: _____.

CHAPTER 9

The People

Explorers

Tic-Tac-Toe Menu

Objectives Covered Through This Menu and These Activities

- Students will examine the traits of explorers and why they choose to explore.
- Students will research and present information on a famous explorer.

Materials Needed by Students for Completion

- Magazines (for collage)
- Scrapbooking materials

Time Frame

- 2 weeks—Students are given the menu as the unit is started. As the teacher presents lessons throughout the week, he or she should refer back to the options associated with that content. The teacher will go over all of the options for that content and have students place check-marks in the boxes that represent the activities they are most interested in completing. As teaching continues over the next 2 weeks, activities chosen and completed should make a column or a row. When students make this pattern, they have completed one activity on the characteristics of explorers, the reasons why they explore, and information on a specific explorer.
- 1 week—At the start of the unit, the teacher chooses the three activities he or she feels are most valuable for the students. Stations can be set up in the classroom. These three activities are available for student choice throughout the week, as regular instruction takes place.
- 1–2 days—The teacher chooses an activity from the menu to use with the entire class.

Suggested Forms

- All-purpose rubric
- Oral report rubric
- Proposal form for projects

Name:_____

Explorers

☐ **Why Explore?** Each explorer has his or her own specific reasons for the journey he or she takes. Usually, however, these reasons can be broken down into general categories. Make a windowpane to show the general reasons explorers go on their journeys.	☐ **Choose Your Own Explorer** Choose an explorer or adventurer and come to class as that person. Be prepared to answer questions about your trip, what happened along the way, and why you decided to go.	☐ **Traits of Explorers** Create a collage of words or quotes that express all of the traits or characteristics of a successful explorer.
☐ **Traits of Explorers** Develop your own song about explorers and what makes an explorer successful.	☐ **Free Choice** (Fill out your proposal form before beginning the free choice!)	☐ **Choose Your Own Explorer** Read a biography about the explorer you have chosen. Create a new book cover for this book.
☐ **Choose Your Own Explorer** Create a scrapbook to document the adventures of the explorer you have chosen.	☐ **Traits of Explorers** Think of one of the great exploration trips in the past. Create an advertisement to recruit explorers for this trip. It should include traits you are looking for in a successful explorer.	☐ **Why Explore?** Choose the one place you would like to visit or explore if you could go anywhere. Why would you want to go to that specific place? Write a letter to your parents explaining where you would like to go and why.

Check the boxes you plan to complete. They should form a tic-tac-toe across or down. All products are due by: _____.

Native Americans

Tic-Tac-Toe Menu

Objectives Covered Through This Menu and These Activities
- Students will investigate areas that were inhabited by Native Americans.
- Students will examine and show examples of Native American culture.
- Students will present information on the different types of Native Americans.

Materials Needed by Students for Completion
- Map of the United States (for color coding Native American regions)
- Microsoft PowerPoint or other slideshow software
- Blank index cards (for how-to card)
- Materials for Native American handicrafts
- Scrapbooking materials

Special Notes on the Use of This Menu
Students do have the option to prepare a food that was eaten by Native Americans. If resources are limited or you are not allowed to have food in the classroom, this option could easily be changed to just research the food and create a recipe from that particular tribe.

Time Frame
- 2 weeks—Students are given the menu as the unit is started. As the teacher presents lessons throughout the week, he or she should refer back to the options associated with that content. The teacher will go over all of the options for that content and have students place checkmarks in the boxes that represent the activities they are most interested in completing. As teaching continues over the next 2 weeks, activities chosen and completed should make a column or a row. When students make this pattern, they have completed one activity from each content area: Native American culture, where and how Native Americans lived, and how groups of Native Americans differed.
- 1 week—At the start of the unit, the teacher chooses the three activities he or she feels are most valuable for the students. Stations can be

set up in the classroom. These three activities are available for student choice throughout the week, as regular instruction takes place.

- 1–2 days—The teacher chooses an activity from the menu to use with the entire class.

Suggested Forms

- All-purpose rubric
- Oral report rubric
- Proposal form for projects

Native Americans

☐ *Locations of Native Americans* Using the map of the United States, color code the areas that were inhabited by large groups of Native Americans.	☐ *Build a Game* Make a popular Native American game and write a how-to card to explain the instructions for its construction.	☐ *Create a Scrapbook* Create a scrapbook for a group of Native Americans that lived near where you live now. Include information on their housing, foods, clothing, family structure, and general living conditions.
☐ *Perform a Legend* Legends are very important to Native Americans. Find one legend that interests you. Change the legend into a play and perform it with the help of your classmates.	☐ **Free Choice** (Fill out your proposal form before beginning the free choice!)	☐ *Prepare a Meal* Research a dish that was typical for the Native Americans in your region. Write the recipe and prepare the food to share with your classmates.
☐ *Create a Handicraft* Create an Native American handicraft of your choice to share with the class. (Examples include cornhusk dolls, dream catchers, beaded bags, rain sticks, and the like.)	☐ *Comparing Native American Groups* Make a Venn diagram to compare and contrast two local Native American groups.	☐ *Types of Native Americans* Create a PowerPoint presentation about the types of Native Americans that lived in your state.

Check the boxes you plan to complete. They should form a tic-tac-toe across or down. All products are due by: _____.

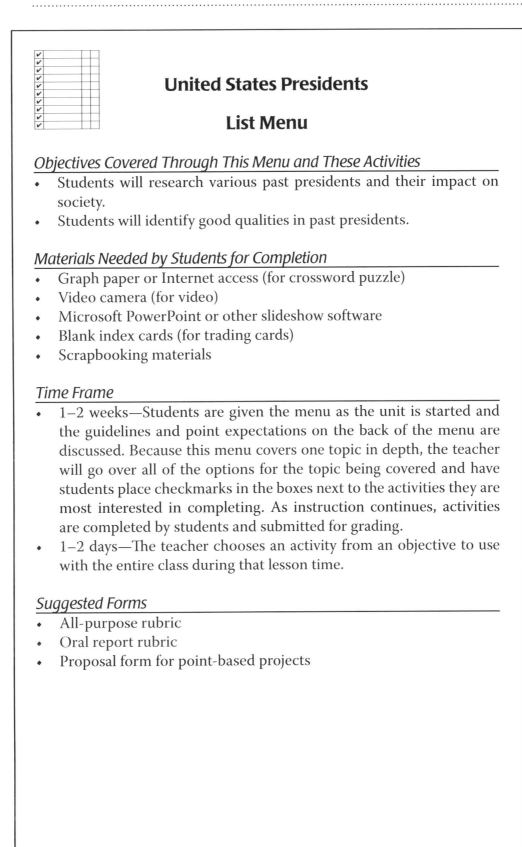

United States Presidents

List Menu

Objectives Covered Through This Menu and These Activities

- Students will research various past presidents and their impact on society.
- Students will identify good qualities in past presidents.

Materials Needed by Students for Completion

- Graph paper or Internet access (for crossword puzzle)
- Video camera (for video)
- Microsoft PowerPoint or other slideshow software
- Blank index cards (for trading cards)
- Scrapbooking materials

Time Frame

- 1–2 weeks—Students are given the menu as the unit is started and the guidelines and point expectations on the back of the menu are discussed. Because this menu covers one topic in depth, the teacher will go over all of the options for the topic being covered and have students place checkmarks in the boxes next to the activities they are most interested in completing. As instruction continues, activities are completed by students and submitted for grading.
- 1–2 days—The teacher chooses an activity from an objective to use with the entire class during that lesson time.

Suggested Forms

- All-purpose rubric
- Oral report rubric
- Proposal form for point-based projects

Name:_____

United States Presidents Challenge Investigation

Guidelines:

1. You may complete as many of the activities listed as you would like within the time period given.
2. You may choose any combination of activities.
3. Your goal is 100 points. You may earn up to _____ points in extra credit.
4. You may be as creative as you like within the guidelines listed below.
5. You must show your plan to your teacher by _____.
6. Activities may be turned in at any time during the working time period. They will be graded and recorded on this sheet as you continue to work, so keep it safe!

Plan to Do	Activity to Complete	Point Value	Date Completed	Points Earned
	Choose the president that you feel has had the greatest impact on the United States. Come to class as that president and talk about your accomplishments.	30		
	Create a PowerPoint presentation about the life of a president of your choice.	20		
	A book is being written about the vice presidents who stepped into office when the president could no longer complete his duty. Create a book cover for this new book.	25		
	Create an American president crossword puzzle.	15		
	Complete another student's president crossword puzzle.	10		
	Make a brochure detailing what it takes to be a good president. Include examples from our past presidents to prove your point.	30		
	Create a set of trading cards for 10 of your favorite presidents. Include a picture, a brief biography, and each person's greatest accomplishment while in office.	30		
	Make an acrostic for the first and last name of a president of your choice. Include biographical information for each letter of his name.	20		
	Design a scrapbook to reflect the life of one of the presidents before, during, and after his time in that role.	20		
	Choose the president that you believe has had the greatest impact on our state. Write and perform a song that shares what the president did to have such an impact.	30		
	Create a video to share facts about our presidents.	20		
	Create a U.S. presidents board game. Incorporate at least 10 presidents in the game.	25		
	Total number of points you are planning to earn.		**Total points earned:**	

I am planning to complete _____ activities that could earn up to a total of _____ points.

Teacher's initials _____ Student's signature _____

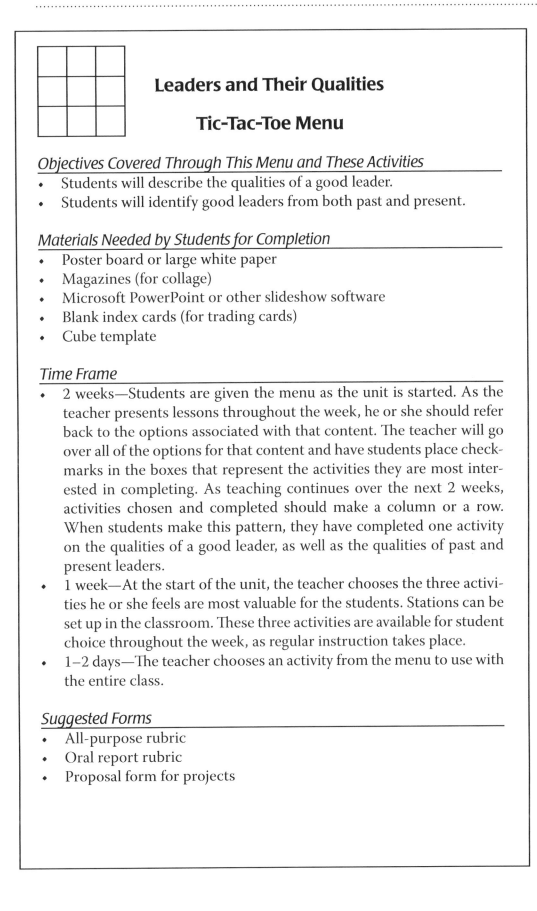

Leaders and Their Qualities

Tic-Tac-Toe Menu

Objectives Covered Through This Menu and These Activities
- Students will describe the qualities of a good leader.
- Students will identify good leaders from both past and present.

Materials Needed by Students for Completion
- Poster board or large white paper
- Magazines (for collage)
- Microsoft PowerPoint or other slideshow software
- Blank index cards (for trading cards)
- Cube template

Time Frame
- 2 weeks—Students are given the menu as the unit is started. As the teacher presents lessons throughout the week, he or she should refer back to the options associated with that content. The teacher will go over all of the options for that content and have students place checkmarks in the boxes that represent the activities they are most interested in completing. As teaching continues over the next 2 weeks, activities chosen and completed should make a column or a row. When students make this pattern, they have completed one activity on the qualities of a good leader, as well as the qualities of past and present leaders.
- 1 week—At the start of the unit, the teacher chooses the three activities he or she feels are most valuable for the students. Stations can be set up in the classroom. These three activities are available for student choice throughout the week, as regular instruction takes place.
- 1–2 days—The teacher chooses an activity from the menu to use with the entire class.

Suggested Forms
- All-purpose rubric
- Oral report rubric
- Proposal form for projects

Leaders and Their Qualities

☐ **What Is a Good Leader?** Using a magazine, create a collage of words that show the qualities of a good leader.	☐ **Qualities of Past Leaders** Create a PowerPoint presentation of people who were leaders in our country. Devote one slide to each leader and the qualities he or she possessed.	☐ **Qualities of Present Leaders** Develop a questionnaire to determine what other people think are good qualities of our present leaders. Use the questionnaire to gather information from 10 people. Present your questionnaire and results in a report.
☐ **Qualities of Past Leaders** Think about leaders from the past and choose the one you think has had the greatest impact on the United States. Create a song about this leader and his or her qualities that created change.	☐ **Free Choice** (Fill out your proposal form before beginning the free choice!)	☐ **What Is a Good Leader?** Make a poster of a good leader. Show all the characteristics he or she should possess.
☐ **Qualities of Present Leaders** Create a set of trading cards of people you believe are good leaders. The cards should include photos or drawings, the qualities that make them good leaders, and their impact on society.	☐ **What Is a Good Leader?** Create a leader cube to be used as a game. Each side should have a situation where a person is either being a good or a poor leader. Your classmates can roll the cube and tell whether the person is a good or poor leader.	☐ **Qualities of Past Leaders** Choose a person who was a leader of our country. Create an acrostic for his or her first and last name. For each letter, record a characteristic that helped to make that person a great leader.

Check the boxes you plan to complete. They should form a tic-tac-toe across or down.
All products are due by: _____.

Leader Cube

Complete the cube for leadership qualities. Each side should have a situation where a person is either being a good or poor leader. Your classmates can roll the cube and tell whether the person is a good or poor leader. Use this pattern or create your own cube.

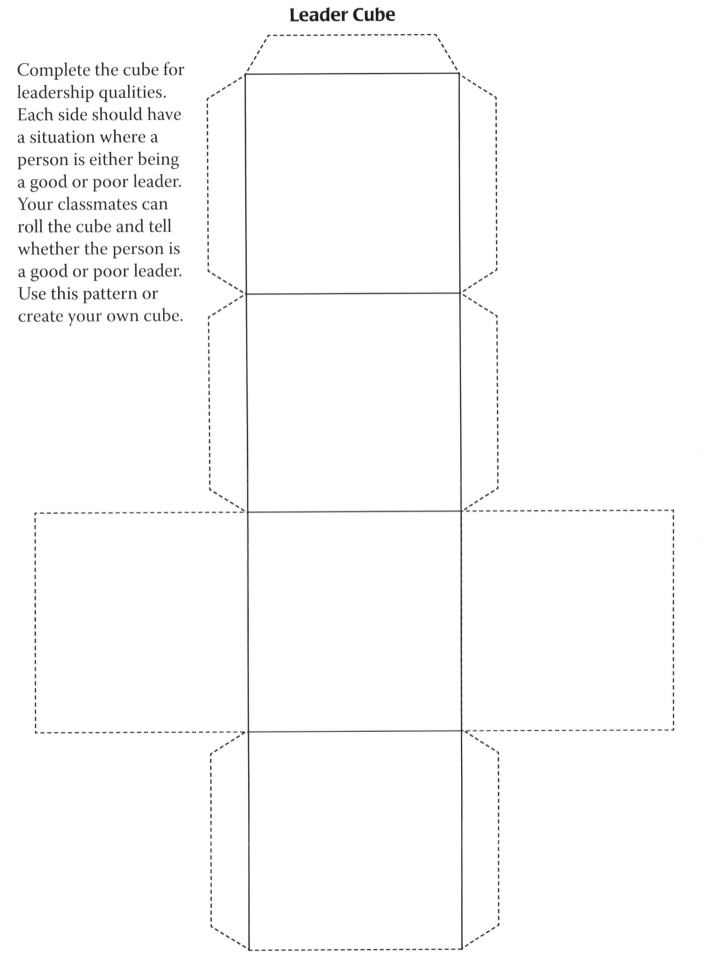

Citizenship

Tic-Tac-Toe Menu

Objectives Covered Through This Menu and These Activities
- Students will identify and explain the qualities and responsibilities of a good citizen.
- Students will give examples of good citizens.

Materials Needed by Students for Completion
- Poster board or large white paper
- Microsoft PowerPoint or other slideshow software
- Blank index cards (for trading cards)

Time Frame
- 2 weeks—Students are given the menu as the unit is started. As the teacher presents lessons throughout the week, he or she should refer back to the options associated with that content. The teacher will go over all of the options for that content and have students place checkmarks in the boxes that represent the activities they are most interested in completing. As teaching continues over the next 2 weeks, activities chosen and completed should make a column or a row. When students make this pattern, they have completed one activity from each of the focus areas.
- 1 week—At the start of the unit, the teacher chooses the three activities he or she feels are most valuable for the students. Stations can be set up in the classroom. These three activities are available for student choice throughout the week, as regular instruction takes place.
- 1–2 days—The teacher chooses an activity from the menu to use with the entire class.

Suggested Forms
- All-purpose rubric
- Oral report rubric
- Proposal form for projects

Name:_____

Citizenship

☐ **Responsibilities of Good Citizens** Write a story about a person your age who takes on the responsibilities of a good citizen even though it isn't the easiest choice for him or her.	☐ **Who Are Good Citizens?** Choose someone famous who you think is a good citizen. Come to class as that person and talk about what makes a good citizen.	☐ **Qualities of Good Citizens** Create a good-citizen quiz for your classmates. The quiz should test them to see if they know the qualities of good citizens.
☐ **Qualities of Good Citizens** Write and perform a play that shows both good and poor citizens. Be creative in the qualities you choose to show.	☐ **Free Choice** (Fill out your proposal form before beginning the free choice!)	☐ **Who Are Good Citizens?** Create a set of trading cards of famous people who are good citizens. The cards should include the characteristics they have that make them good citizens.
☐ **Who Are Good Citizens?** Create a PowerPoint presentation of good citizens. Gather photos and information on famous people that you believe are good citizens. Each slide should discuss why that person is a good citizen.	☐ **Qualities of Good Citizens** Create a poster of a good citizen. Show at least 10 characteristics a good citizen would have or show.	☐ **Responsibilities of Good Citizens** Create a brochure that shares the responsibilities of a good citizen.

Check the boxes you plan to complete. They should form a tic-tac-toe across or down.
All products are due by: _____.

Cultures

Game Show Menu

Objectives Covered Through This Menu and These Activities
- Students will identify and share traditions and celebrations of their culture.
- Students will explain the history of their culture.
- Students will investigate the food, arts, music, and writings from their culture.

Materials Needed by Students for Completion
- Poster board or large white paper
- Materials for board games (e.g., folders, colored cards, etc.)
- Food for cultural feast
- Materials for student-created models (for instruments)
- Video camera (for news report and documentary)
- String (for mobile)
- Microsoft PowerPoint or other slideshow software
- Blank index cards (for recipe box and trading cards)
- Scrapbooking materials

Special Notes on the Use of This Menu
One of the products students can choose is a cultural feast. This is a wonderful activity when all of the students bring food on the same day. If you choose to allow the large feast, remember to always have the ingredients posted so that students with certain allergies can identify foods they should avoid.

Time Frame
- 2–3 weeks—Students are given the menu as the unit is started and the guidelines and point expectations on the back of the menu are discussed. As lessons are taught throughout the unit, students and the teacher can refer back to the options associated with that topic. The teacher will go over all of the options for the topic being covered and have students place checkmarks in the boxes next to the activities they are most interested in completing. As teaching continues over next 2–3 weeks, activities are discussed, chosen, and submitted for grading.

- 1 week—At the beginning of the unit, the teacher chooses an activity from each area that he or she feels would be most valuable for the students. Stations can be set up in the classroom. These activities are available for student choice throughout the week, as regular instruction takes place.
- 1–2 days—The teacher chooses an activity from an objective to use with the entire class during that lesson time.

Suggested Forms

- All-purpose rubric
- Oral report rubric
- Student-taught lesson rubric
- Proposal form for point-based projects

Guidelines for Cultures Game Show Menu

- You must choose at least one activity from each topic area.
- You may not do more than two activities in any one topic area for credit. (You are, of course, welcome to do more than two for your own investigation.)
- Grading will be ongoing, so turn in products as you complete them.
- All free-choice proposals must be turned in and approved *prior* to working on that free choice.
- You must earn 120 points for a 100%. You may earn extra credit up to _____ points.
- You must show your plan for completion by: _____.

Name:_____

Cultures

Celebrations	Traditions	History	Art	Authors	Music	Edible Culture	Points for Each Level
☐ Create a windowpane for the different celebrations of your culture. (10 pts.)	☐ Make a set of trading cards about the traditions of your culture. (10 pts.)	☐ Make a timeline that shows the history of your culture. (10 pts.)	☐ Create a brochure for an art gallery showing art from your culture. (10 pts.)	☐ Make a flipbook for the well-known authors of your culture. Include the names of works they have written. (10 pts.)	☐ Research the music of your culture and collect samples to share with your classmates. (15 pts.)	☐ Make a recipe box of at least five traditional recipes common in your culture. (10 pts.)	10–15 points
☐ Make a video documentary that details the different celebrations of your culture. (25 pts.)	☐ Create a Venn diagram to compare your own traditions to that of another culture. (20 pts.)	☐ Prepare a scrapbook that shares the history of your culture. (25 pts.)	☐ Create a PowerPoint presentation that shares the art of your culture. Include how the art is a reflection of the culture. (25 pts.)	☐ Change one of your culture's stories into a play and perform it for your classmates. (25 pts.)	☐ Make a poster that shows the type of music used by your culture, as well as how the music is produced. (20 pts.)	☐ Make a game to test your classmates' knowledge of the types of food your culture eats. (25 pts.)	20–25 points
☐ Create a celebration for your classmates based on your culture. Be as authentic as possible. (30 pts.)	☐ Prepare a news report on the most important tradition of your culture. Be creative in your presentation. (30 pts.)	☐ Who had the biggest impact on the history of your culture? Come to class as this person and be prepared to share your impact on the culture. (30 pts.)	☐ Using similar mediums, create your own art in the style of your culture. (30 pts.)	☐ Design a lesson for your classmates on various important authors found within your culture. (30 pts.)	☐ Build an instrument and create your own song in the style of your culture. (30 pts.)	☐ Create a cultural feast for your class. Prepare at least three dishes from your culture and share. (30 pts.)	30 points
Free Choice (prior approval) **(25–50 pts.)**	**Free Choice** (prior approval) **(25–50 pts.)**	**Free Choice** (prior approval) **(25–50 pts.)**	**Free Choice** (prior approval) **(25–50 pts.)**	**Free Choice** (prior approval) **(25–50 pts.)**	**Free Choice** (prior approval) **(25–50 pts.)**	**Free Choice** (prior approval) **(25–50 pts.)**	25–50 points
Total:	Total:	Total:	Total:	Total:	Total:	Total:	Total Grade:

CHAPTER 10

Geography

Maps and Globes

List Menu

Objectives Covered Through This Menu and These Activities

- Students will create maps of local areas that include all necessary components.
- Students will investigate how different maps are created.
- Students will compare different types of maps.
- Students will use latitude and longitude to locate items on a map or globe.

Materials Needed by Students for Completion

- Poster board or large white paper
- Materials for board games (e.g., folders, colored cards, etc.)
- Materials for student-created models (for homemade compass)
- Microsoft PowerPoint or other slideshow software
- Materials for three-dimensional map

Time Frame

- 1–2 weeks—Students are given the menu as the unit is started and the guidelines and point expectations are discussed. Because this menu covers one topic in depth, the teacher will go over all of the options on the menu and have students place checkmarks in the boxes next to the activities they are most interested in completing. As instruction continues, activities are completed by students and submitted for grading.
- 1–2 days—The teacher chooses an activity from an objective to use with the entire class during lesson time.

Suggested Forms

- All-purpose rubric
- Proposal form for point-based projects

Name:_____

Maps and Globes Challenge Investigation

Guidelines:

1. You may complete as many of the activities listed as you would like within the time period given.
2. You may choose any combination of activities.
3. Your goal is 100 points. You may earn up to _____ points in extra credit.
4. You may be as creative as you like within the guidelines listed below.
5. You must show your plan to your teacher by _____.
6. Activities may be turned in at any time during the working time period. They will be graded and recorded on this sheet as you continue to work, so keep it safe!

Plan to Do	Activity to Complete	Point Value	Date Completed	Points Earned
	Create a three-dimensional map of your playground. Keep everything to scale, and provide the scale and an appropriate legend for your map.	25		
	Research how scientists map the bottom of the ocean. Make a poster that shows how this is done.	15		
	Draw a map of your neighborhood with a legend that includes proper scale.	20		
	Create a how-to brochure that shows how to determine the latitude and longitude of a location using a map or a globe.	20		
	Using a Venn diagram, compare a Mercator map to another type of map of your choice.	20		
	Create a scavenger hunt across the globe. Have your readers find at least seven locations based on latitude and longitude and answer questions about each location they find.	25		
	Build a homemade compass and write directions for its use.	25		
	Design a poster that shows your own map symbols for landmarks and types of roads near where you live.	20		
	Create a PowerPoint presentation on the different types of maps and the symbols used on each.	15		
	Make a map-based board game where students travel the globe answering questions about maps.	25		
	Free choice: Must be outlined on a proposal form and approved before beginning work.	15–30		
	Total number of points you are planning to earn.		**Total points earned:**	

I am planning to complete _____ activities that could earn up to a total of _____ points.

Teacher's initials _____ Student's signature _____

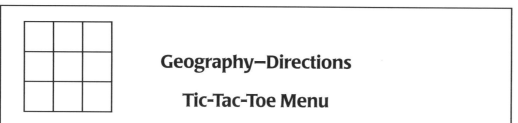

Geography–Directions

Tic-Tac-Toe Menu

Objectives Covered Through This Menu and These Activities

- Students will locate and name the 50 states and their capitals.
- Students will use both immediate and cardinal directions.

Materials Needed by Students for Completion

- Graph paper or Internet access (for crossword puzzle)
- Microsoft PowerPoint or other slideshow software
- Blank index cards (for concentration card game)

Time Frame

- 2 weeks—Students are given the menu as the unit is started. As the teacher presents lessons throughout the week, he or she should refer back to the options associated with that content. The teacher will go over all of the options for that content and have students place checkmarks in the boxes that represent the activities they are most interested in completing. As teaching continues over the next 2 weeks, activities chosen and completed should make a column or a row. When students make this pattern, they have completed one activity from each focus area.
- 1 week—At the start of the unit, the teacher chooses the three activities he or she feels are most valuable for the students. Stations can be set up in the classroom. These three activities are available for student choice throughout the week, as regular instruction takes place.
- 1–2 days—The teacher chooses an activity from the menu to use with the entire class.

Suggested Forms

- All-purpose rubric
- Student-taught lesson rubric
- Oral report rubric
- Proposal form for projects

Name:_____

Geography—Directions

☐ **States and Capitals** Create a concentration game to help you remember the states and their capitals. USA	☐ **Cardinal Directions** Write directions from the front of the school to the playground using only cardinal directions and the number of steps.	☐ **Immediate Directions** Draw a map that shows how you get to school every morning. Write the directions to go from home to school.
☐ **Cardinal Directions** Develop a lesson to teach your classmates about cardinal directions. Be ready to present this to your classmates.	☐ **Free Choice** (Fill out your proposal form before beginning the free choice!)	☐ **States and Capitals** Create a crossword puzzle for the 20 capitals you have the most trouble remembering.
☐ **Immediate Directions** Create a Simon Says Scavenger Hunt for your playground. Start by the door and give directions and number of footsteps to find at least three important features in the playground area.	☐ **States and Capitals** Create a PowerPoint presentation for the 20 capitals you have the most difficulty remembering. Include a picture or way to help you remember its state.	☐ **Cardinal Directions** Create a worksheet about cardinal directions and how to use them.

Check the boxes you plan to complete. They should form a tic-tac-toe across or down. All products are due by: _____.

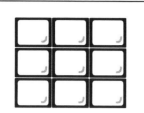

American Landmarks and Symbols

Game Show Menu

Objectives Covered Through This Menu and These Activities
- Students will understand the historic significance of American landmarks and symbols.
- Students will identify historic landmarks and symbols.

Materials Needed by Students for Completion
- Poster board or large white paper
- Graph paper or Internet access (for crossword puzzle)
- Materials for student-created models (for White House model)
- Magazines (for collage)
- Video camera (for news report)
- Microsoft PowerPoint or other slideshow software
- Shoe boxes (for dioramas)
- Cube template

Time Frame
- 2–3 weeks—Students are given the menu as the unit is started and the guidelines and point expectations on the back of the menu are discussed. As lessons are taught throughout the unit, students and the teacher can refer back to the options associated with that topic. The teacher will go over all of the options for the topic being covered and have students place checkmarks in the boxes next to the activities they are most interested in completing. As teaching continues over next 2–3 weeks, activities are discussed, chosen, and submitted for grading.
- 1 week—At the beginning of the unit, the teacher chooses an activity from each area that he or she feels would be most valuable for the students. Stations can be set up in the classroom. These activities are available for student choice throughout the week, as regular instruction takes place.
- 1–2 days—The teacher chooses an activity from an objective to use with the entire class during that lesson time.

Suggested Forms
- All-purpose rubric
- Oral report rubric
- Proposal form for point-based projects
- $1 contract (for diorama)

Guidelines for American Landmarks and Symbols Game Show Menu

- You must choose at least one activity from each topic area.
- You may not do more than two activities in any one topic area for credit. (You are, of course, welcome to do more than two for your own investigation.)
- Grading will be ongoing, so turn in products as you complete them.
- All free-choice proposals must be turned in and approved *prior* to working on that free choice.
- You must earn 120 points for a 100%. You may earn extra credit up to _____ points.
- You must show your plan for completion by: _____.

American Landmarks and Symbols

Name:_____

Statue of Liberty	The White House	The American Flag	The Star Spangled Banner	Local Landmarks	State Landmarks	Points for Each Level
☐ Create an informational poster about the Statue of Liberty. (10 pts.)	☐ Create a crossword puzzle about the White House. (10 pts.)	☐ Create a project cube that answers important questions about our flag. (10 pts.)	☐ Sing the first and second verse of the Star Spangled Banner for your teacher. (15 pts.)	☐ Draw a map that shows local landmarks. (10 pts.)	☐ Locate state landmarks on a state map and note their significance. (15 pts.)	10–15 points
☐ Create a travel advertisement for the Statue of Liberty. Include its history and why tourists may wish to see it. (20 pts.)	☐ Create a book cover for a book about the history of the White House. (20 pts.)	☐ Write and perform a play that tells the story of the creation of the first American flag. (25 pts.)	☐ Create a diorama to show the situation described in the Star Spangled Banner. (20 pts.)	☐ Create brochure for a local landmark of your choice. Include its history, significance to the state, and why people may want to visit it. (25 pts.)	☐ Create a PowerPoint presentation that shares at least five state landmarks. Include each one's location and significance in history. (25 pts.)	20–25 points
☐ The Statue of Liberty has become a symbol of freedom to many Americans. Write a story that tells how things may have been different if we had not received the statue. (30 pts.)	☐ There has been more than one White House built, each better than the one before it. Examine the layout and structure of our present White House and create a model to propose changes you would suggest to make it better and safer. (30 pts.)	☐ In the past, certain groups have chosen to burn the American flag. Do you agree that there are times when this is appropriate? Prepare a speech sharing your point of view on this issue. (30 pts.)	☐ Write a letter to a pen pal in another country about our country's national anthem, its importance, and what it means to you. (30 pts.)	☐ There are local, state, and national landmarks. Choose a landmark close to you and write a letter to the national committee explaining why your landmark is important enough to be considered for national status. (30 pts.)	☐ Choose a state landmark you think is important. Pretend you are at that spot when it became historically famous. Create a news report about what happened there. (30 pts.)	30 points
Free Choice (prior approval) (25–50 pts.)	Free Choice (prior approval) (25–50 pts.)	Free Choice (prior approval) (25–50 pts.)	Free Choice (prior approval) (25–50 pts.)	Free Choice (prior approval) (25–50 pts.)	Free Choice (prior approval) (25–50 pts.)	25–50 points
Total:	Total:	Total:	Total:	Total:	Total:	Total Grade:

Our Flag Cube

Complete the cube to answer questions about our flag. Use this pattern or create your own cube.

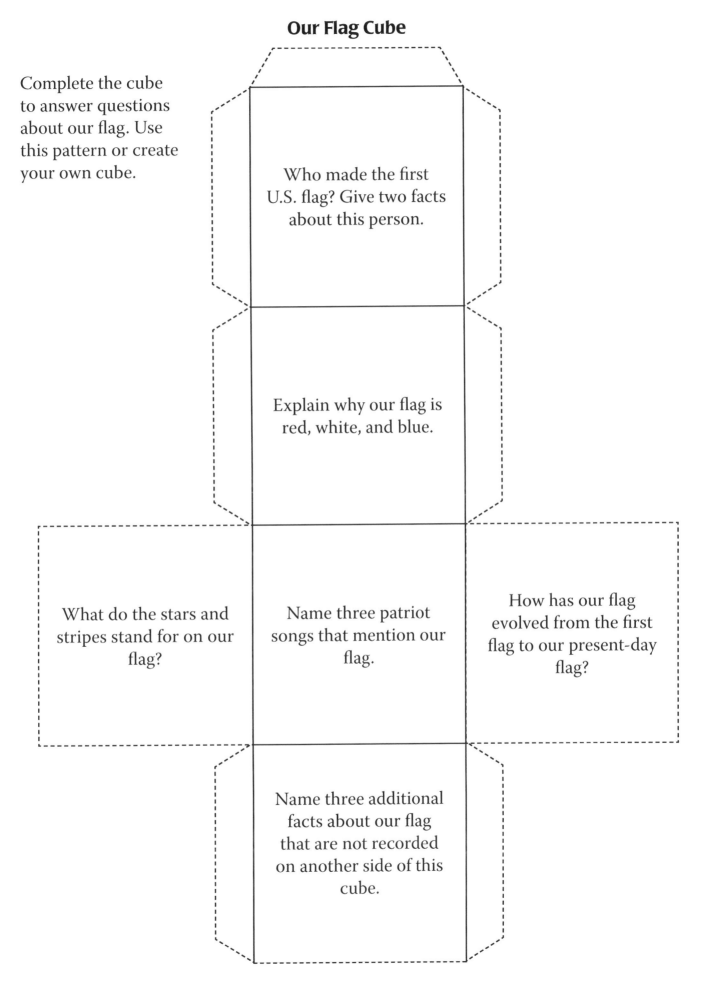

Who made the first U.S. flag? Give two facts about this person.

Explain why our flag is red, white, and blue.

What do the stars and stripes stand for on our flag?

Name three patriot songs that mention our flag.

How has our flag evolved from the first flag to our present-day flag?

Name three additional facts about our flag that are not recorded on another side of this cube.

References

Anderson, L. (Ed.), Krathwohl, D. (Ed.), Airasian, P., Cruikshank, K., Mayer, R., Pintrich, P., et al. (2001). *A taxonomy for learning, teaching, and assessing: A revision of Bloom's taxonomy of educational objectives* (Complete ed.). New York: Longman.

Keen, D. (2001). *Talent in the new millennium: Report on year one of the programme.* Retrieved November 27, 2006, from http://www.dce.ac.nz/research/content_talent.htm

Resources

Dickens, C. (1981). *Oliver Twist.* New York: Bantam Books. (Original work published 1838)

Korman, G. (1984). *No coins, please.* New York: Scholastic.

Merrill, J. (1972). *The toothpaste millionaire.* Boston: Houghton Mifflin.

Paterson, K. (1992). *Lyddie.* New York: Puffin Books.

Wisler, G. C. (1997). *Mustang flats.* New York: Lodestar.

About the Author

After living in the small town of Roscommon, MI, and attending Grand Valley State University, Laurie met a goal she set for herself during her freshman year of high school and began her teaching career by teaching science overseas for 5 years in American schools in both Mexico and Brazil. After returning to the U.S., she taught middle school advanced-level science for 9 years in Houston, TX, before taking a position in the school district's gifted office as a master teacher. This is where she found her true calling—working with the teachers of gifted students, presenting practical, hands-on staff development, and helping teachers develop lessons that better meet the academic needs of our gifted children. Currently, she is a full-time independent gifted and science consultant, traveling throughout the state of Texas providing staff development for teachers of the gifted and administrators, as well as helping school districts meet their science needs.